THE
WILD
WILD
EAST

THE WILD WILD EAST

Lessons for Success in Business in Contemporary Capitalist China

ALAN REFKIN AND DANIEL BORGIA, PhD

iUniverse, Inc.
Bloomington

THE WILD, WILD EAST
LESSONS FOR SUCCESS IN BUSINESS
IN CONTEMPORARY CAPITALIST CHINA

iUniverse books may be ordered through booksellers or by contacting:

iUniverse
1663 Liberty Drive
Bloomington, IN 47403
www.iuniverse.com
1-800-Authors (1-800-288-4677)

ISBN: 978-1-4620-4054-4 (sc)
ISBN: 978-1-4620-4435-1 (ebk)

Library of Congress Control Number: 2011913385

Printed in the United States of America

iUniverse rev. date: 08/18/2011

Alan Refkin:

I would like to dedicate this book to my wife, Marti, my best friend and soul mate.

Dr. Borgia:

I would like to dedicate this book to my wife, Jia Borgia, for her inspiration and for introducing me to China and the Chinese culture.

Table of Contents

Foreword

China today is arguably the most exciting and rapidly changing country in the world—socially, culturally, and, of course, economically. As a result, life in modern China is often full of paradox, and it's becoming increasingly so in this era of unprecedented socioeconomic transformation. In cities throughout China, it still is not unusual to see old men piloting mule-driven carts laden with produce alongside brand-new BMW, Audi, and Mercedes sedans.

Relentless change—so palpably demonstrated by the recently completed Three Gorges Dam project and the resulting relocation of entire cities and their populations—has been an elemental part of China's modern character. China's rice paddies may have sprouted metropolises and manufacturing centers, and its streets may be clogged with cars and pollution, but the people remain rooted in a resonant cultural heritage. Many Chinese still burn *joss* sticks and consult *feng shui* experts for good luck in a new enterprise—even as they negotiate the details of that business opportunity on a cell phone.

Exploding economic prosperity brought about by increasing openness to the outside world during the past thirty years has made this transformation inevitable. China's infrastructure and cities are being rebuilt and modernized—Beijing, Shanghai, and Shenzhen arguably are the most dynamic cities in the world today. China's ascension as a member of the World Trade Organization (WTO) in 2001 underscored its economic emergence and helped to enhance its global political standing as an emerging superpower. The 2008 Olympic Games—China's official "coming out" party—were recently held in Beijing. The globally recognized success and excellence of the Games proved to the world that China is a world power and truly has arrived.

This incredible dynamism extends to evolution and development of China's business landscape as well. Unfortunately, China's rapid opening and expansion of trade has sometimes resulted in widely reported scandals such as the tainted pet food, dry milk, and the lead-painted-toy episodes. But drawing conclusions from a few (though serious) stories about the danger of a few Chinese products would be a mistake. The truth is that the vast majority of the billions of products imported from China and sold in the United States and in other countries around the world is safe and inexpensive and has helped average Americans improve their standard of living by reducing the amount of disposable income they have to spend on everything from clothing to electronics.

There have been other, albeit less publicized, stories about businesspeople who have ventured to China in search of their fortunes—not unlike the pioneers who headed west during the California gold rush to seek theirs. But like the many adventurers who failed to find the mother lode and strike it rich a century and a half ago, making a fortune in China is no easy task. Certainly there are opportunities in China—but there are significant risks in doing business in China as well. Although China is rapidly changing and modernizing, business practices are still deeply rooted in ancient cultural traditions. To be successful, Western businessmen who want to do business in China have to understand the *Chinese way* of doing business—and that's what this book is about.

This story is a chronicle of the life and times of an American financier in today's capitalist China during the past five years. Financial consultant Alan Refkin assisted in taking a Chinese company through the process and preparation required for a public listing on the US capital markets. Although the names of the firms and individuals discussed and described in the story have been disguised—the story is entirely true. Throughout the story, Alan shares his cultural insights about doing business in China through what he has called his "Refkin's Rules."

We hope you enjoy the story.

Daniel J. Borgia, PhD.
Associate Professor of Finance
2002–03 China Fulbright Scholar
University of Nottingham, Ningbo, China

Preface

Dan and I first met when he was the Director of the Florida Gulf Coast University Institute of Chinese Studies. At that time I was traveling to China every few weeks, and Dan and I immediately became close friends, talking about our business dealings and experiences in China. During one of our frequent lunches we decided to write this book together to give the foreign businessman in China more of a level playing field. Dan and I were convinced that if someone had the knowledge that we'd accumulated from our many trips and business dealings in China, they could avoid the steep learning curve we went through and accelerate their success.

When you're conducting business in China you sometimes feel that someone put you in an alternate universe. Past business experiences and methods of conducting business often are of little use in this new environment. You're at a disadvantage as soon as you get off the plane, and it only gets worse after that. To achieve your objectives you'll have to learn a whole new skill set, and you'll have to do it in relatively short order. Of course I didn't know this when I first went to China. The history, the culture, and the geniality of your hosts give one a false sense of security. In China you see what your Chinese client or counterpart wants you to see. Image is as important to the Chinese as reality. In a great many situations they're interchangeable, causing you to feel that you're on equal or better footing than the Chinese businessman sitting across from you, and that the geniality and image of the business presented is genuine and will lead to a successful transaction for both sides. That's not always the case. Negotiating and achieving your objectives takes an understanding of the many facets of Chinese culture and business. I've summarized these facets of Chinese culture and business into "Refkin's Rules." If you apply these rules, I believe that you'll have the understanding and the ability to successfully compete and prosper in the world's second largest economy and avoid the pitfalls so common in Chinese transactions.

As you read this book you might get the impression that Dan and I are not advocates of doing business in China. That's not the case. We believe that, given an understanding of the Chinese and their business practices and culture, that it's highly probable that you'll be successful in China. This book will give you that understanding.

Alan Refkin

CHAPTER 1 ═══════

I Never Wanted to Go to China in the First Place

Like most people who have never visited China, I had only vague impressions of this vast country and ancient culture—accumulated over a lifetime of reading books and newspapers and from watching documentaries, movies, and TV news. Until a few years ago, like most Americans, I thought of China mainly as a tourist destination, conjuring images of the Great Wall of China, Tiananmen Square, and the Forbidden City. I also thought of China as a country with an enormous population and immense manufacturing capabilities where large companies went to get their widgets manufactured cheaply.

But I didn't deal in manufacturing, and I wasn't much of a tourist. I was an experienced financial consultant, and I enjoyed my work. Although I'd done consulting in most areas of the world, I'd never had the opportunity—or the desire, for that matter—to work with clients in China or anywhere else in Asia. Contributing to the general sense of unease I had about doing business in China were the many newspaper and magazine articles I read about how the Chinese had a different set of values than those of us in the West, how you couldn't depend on a written contract or the rule of law; and how Chinese businessmen would hide information from you and deceive you, all with unfailing politeness.

I had also heard many stories and read numerous accounts about the large number of Western businessmen who came to China with great expectations of making insanely profitable investments—but who, in the end, wound up leaving not only without their profits but without their original capital as well. Even more disconcerting, I had heard that in cases where business agreements and contracts with Chinese firms were contested, it was rare for a Western company to prevail in a Chinese court. In the unlikely event that the foreign company did prevail, I understood that it was difficult if not impossible to get the judgment enforced. Because of these stories—and for a number of other reasons—before early 2003 I had never really given much thought to doing business in China.

All of this played heavily on my mind when the possibility of getting involved in business in China was first presented to me. At the time I was happy, successful, and in my mid-fifties. Up to that point, the only Chinese I really wanted to experience was the food I ordered at our favorite Chinese takeout. When someone spoke to me about business in China, I viewed it as someone else's opportunity, and I would retreat into my own thoughts about the company in Germany I was working with that needed financing or the firm in Canada that I was merging with a client. China simply was not relevant to my life. All of that changed in early 2003 when I ran into my good friend Ken Li at a business conference in Boca Raton, Florida.

Ken lives with his wife, Vivian, and their daughter in Boston. Ken and his wife were both born in Hainan, a large island off the southern coast of China, and migrated to the United States when they both were young. Vivian is a world-class acupuncturist and holistic medicine expert while Ken is a financial consultant who works with Western investors who wish to acquire or create joint ventures with firms in China. Ken and Vivian are polar opposites. Ken is very laid-back, always happy and joking—more often laughing at himself than at others. Vivian is more serious and is a focused and caring professional. When my wife Debbie had breast cancer, Vivian took time off from her insanely busy schedule and traveled to Florida with an armload of holistic medicines to help ease the pain of her chemotherapy.

While they were in Florida, Ken and I caught up with each other over coffee and discussed our lives, families, and various business activities. During our chat, I told Ken that I'd been spending a lot of my time working with companies in Latin America and Europe, but was really getting fed up with all of the travel that was required. I told him that I wanted to start concentrating on working with US companies so I could spend more time with my wife and also get my ever-increasing golf handicap under control.

Ken either didn't hear me or completely ignored what I was telling him because he immediately proceeded to ask if I'd ever thought about doing business in China.

Based on past conversations with him, I knew that Ken spent about half of his time in China and that it was common for him to come across transactions that—for a variety of reasons—he was not capable of handling on his own. He knew that because of my experience and industry connections, I could provide him with the resources and expertise he needed to execute some of the larger and more complex transactions that he was reluctant but obligated to turn away. I replied to Ken, as I had repeated in similar past conversations that I still didn't know a damn thing about China other than that my wife and I usually ended up ordering Chinese food before we went to church group on Sunday nights. I also told him that despite the potential, I still had no desire to work in China for all the reasons I'd been told or had read about. All I knew about China was that Chinese people eat very strange food and sometimes make strange noises, and that if you did business over there, you'd certainly get cheated! But this conversation was really nothing new—we had hashed this out in the past. And like I said, I really wasn't interested in China. This was simply Starbucks coffee banter that we both knew would end when the conference ended and I went back home.

Ken laughed and said that, yes, the Chinese did eat strange food, and that, yes, there were some companies and businessmen in China that did take advantage of inexperienced and naive Westerners. However, Ken said, the growth that was taking place in China was so amazing and so vast and so rapid that there were opportunities for investment there that would certainly never happen again in our lifetimes. He also noted—in his commonly jovial manner—that he'd never personally been cheated in China.

Ken said that the investment climate in China, like everything else there, was changing fast—and changing for the better. He said that today the Chinese government was actively and openly encouraging Westerners to invest in Chinese companies and that investment in China was becoming more mainstream—reliable, predictable, and, yes, Western. Ken rightly argued that because China was home to a quarter of the world's population and because it would continue to open to Western business and culture, it was inevitable that this is where the opportunity to make *serious* money would be during the next several decades. Interestingly, he also told me that very few Western investment firms had branched out to China's "second tier" cities, each with populations of millions and where the heaviest growth and greatest opportunities would occur during the coming years. "That's where the treasure is buried," said Ken.

Ken invited me to come with him to China and take a look for myself. "Bring your wife if you want," Ken said. "At the very least, the two of you will get to see the Great Wall of China! What do you have to lose, Alan?!"

But I was still skeptical. As far as I was concerned, China was still like the *Wild, Wild West* in terms of business and investment. "I'll leave the pioneering work to someone else," I thought. I told Ken, "Thanks but no thanks"—I'd still have to pass.

I didn't think anything of our conversation until several months later when I saw Ken again on a business trip to Boston. Because we were such good friends, he and I usually got together for lunch or dinner whenever I was in Boston. During our conversation at dinner, Ken asked me if I'd given any more thought about working with him on business opportunities in China. A little irritated at being hounded, I said that I *still* hadn't changed my mind. "Ken is nothing if not persistent," I thought to myself. Ken laughed and ribbed me about the great, once-in-a-lifetime opportunity I was missing to get involved in the world's biggest business and investment market. "Just wait, you'll really regret this," Ken said. Becoming a bit exasperated, I said, "Ken, let's just enjoy this lobster and talk about the Red Sox." I just wanted to have dinner in peace and talk about the Boston Red Sox, Ken's favorite team and the one subject I could count on that would shift the conversation in another direction. Then to ensure that I had put an end to a conversation that I knew would be recurring, I told Ken that I would go to China with him *only* if he had an outstanding investment opportunity in a Chinese company to work on and *only* if that company was willing to pay all expenses—hotel, meals, business class air tickets, you name it—for both me and my wife. And to make absolutely sure that this trip would never happen and to finally close the book and shut Ken up about me and China, I told him that I would only feel comfortable if two close friends of mine who ran a very large hedge fund (let's call it ABC Capital) could also come along with me. "All expenses paid for everyone!" I bellowed to Ken with a sarcastic smirk on my face. I was sure that the cost of four business class tickets along with the hotel and associated expenses resulting from a week or more touring China would deter any Chinese company from seeking my assistance since—after paying these substantial costs—there was no assurance that I would ever even return.

Incredibly—I thought wrong! Not even a week had passed after leaving Boston before I received a phone call from Ken. He was so excited that he could barely contain himself. Ken said that the Chinese firm he was working with had agreed to pay for ALL expenses—including the business class airfare for four. Ken said that the president and founder of the company was eager to meet us and wanted us to come as soon as possible.

My jaw dropped, and I stared at the phone in disbelief. This was the last thing I expected to hear from Ken. In fact, I didn't expect to hear from him at all about it! During our conversation in Boston I had done some rough mental calculations to get a ballpark idea about what a trip like this would cost, and I had conservatively estimated the price tag to be at least $25,000, considering the cost of the tickets, hotels, meals, transportation, and related expenses. This Chinese company didn't know me from Adam! "Why would they agree to such a ridiculous thing?" I asked myself.

Now that I had painted myself into a box, however, there was no getting out. Besides, I said to myself, "How can I turn down a free business class, all expenses paid vacation to China for me, my wife, and my friends?" Obviously, the Chinese businessman knew that I couldn't when he extended the offer. A moment later, it suddenly dawned on me that, since I really didn't expect to go to China, I hadn't even asked what business the Chinese company that had graciously offered to host us was involved in. I didn't know where the company was located, how old it was, or the background and structure of the firm's owners. I hadn't requested the company's financial statements, nor did I ask even the most basic questions about the business that I normally would have asked prior to speaking with a company that I would consider working with or investing in. "Still," I thought, "there's just *no way* I can turn this down!"

Ken was still excited and babbling on when I interrupted him to ask if he could get me a financial and business package about the company so I could study it prior to our departure. I also told Ken that I would coordinate with my friends at ABC Capital to find out when they might be free to come along (if at all) and to try to plan a mutually agreeable itinerary and then get back to him.

About a week later, Ken sent me an e-mail with the information about the company in China we were going to evaluate. The firm (we'll call it AutoStar) was in the automotive maintenance and repair business. AutoStar was located in Beijing, and it was run by a person who had recently retired from a fairly high position in government service and who had been presented with a top government management award for his long list of accomplishments and service in running government organizations. The financial statements I received indicated that the company was fairly small but that it had experienced substantial growth in revenues and profits each year since it was founded.

In his e-mail, Ken wrote that although the automotive maintenance and repair business was not glamorous, it was booming along with China's rapidly expanding automotive industry. Until a few years ago, very few Chinese owned private cars, and the auto industry was very small in China. In recent years, however, particularly after the price of automobiles began to rapidly drop following China's ascension to the WTO in 2001, private automobile ownership in China has exploded. Over a thousand new cars a day entered Beijing, I was told. Because of this, Ken assured me that this industry was truly a "diamond in the rough"—a low tech business in a high growth market.

Ken also told me that because a consumer-driven auto industry in China was so new, the Chinese automotive repair market was currently highly fragmented. "In China," he said "you're more likely to see a tiny storefront mom and pop repair shop than a large, Western-styled franchise."

To me, this business model seemed to offer a unique opportunity with serious potential. In comparison with the European and American markets, which possess mature auto industries and auto service infrastructures, China's market is still in its infancy. Western markets are much more competitive, and, as a result, profit margins are lower. In the United States and Europe, unless you possess a unique competitive advantage or spend an enormous amount of money on research and development or marketing to differentiate product or service, it's very difficult to earn extraordinary profits. "That's not the way it is in China at all," said Ken. "China's auto industry is new; it's in the early stages of establishing its industrial infrastructure, and so enormous profit margins are there for the taking!"

Ken also said that the Chinese view anything that is made in America to be of the highest quality and prestige and that they are willing to pay a premium for it. "If something is stamped *Made in America*, Chinese consumers understand they are getting a good product—the real thing—no knockoffs," said Ken. "The average Chinese consumer simply doesn't trust in the value or integrity of Chinese-made products or services. How could he?" asked Ken. "China is a country that prided itself on making perfect replicas cheaply!"

A few mornings later, I opened my inbox and saw an e-mail from Ken with a business plan attachment. Up to that point, I had never seen a Chinese business plan. At first glance, I was surprised at its apparent quality. The AutoStar plan seemed to be well presented. It was coherent and filled with colorful photos and graphics describing all aspects of the company. It wasn't perfect—but I'd never seen a perfect plan in all my years in the business. Sure, the forecasts seemed a bit optimistic. But the truth is that I've never had *anyone* send me a business plan that said, "My business is in the tank, and my financial position is bad and may get worse—but I still want you to give me lots of money so I can continue to manage the business and maintain my present extravagant lifestyle." As a financial consultant and as an investor myself, I learned long ago to expect optimistic business plan projections. After getting the plan, I saw it as my job and my responsibility to ask the hard questions to determine which assumptions and projections were reasonable and which weren't. In this case, AutoStar's financial projections seemed to suggest growth potential that would be interesting to explore during our conversations.

One aspect of AutoStar's business plan that was a bit unusual was its presentation. The vast majority of the hundreds of business plans I've reviewed during my career are short on bluster, focusing instead on facts, financials, and other hard content. In contrast, AutoStar's plan was very long on bluster and was grandiose in its presentation, devoting disproportionate emphasis on extolling the virtues and accomplishments of its founder and CEO, Mr. Wong. This brings me to the first of my "Refkin's Rules" for doing business in China that I will introduce throughout this book.[1]

Refkin's Rule #1: Remember the importance of *face*.

In China, always remember the importance of "face" in the conduct of all of your personal and business relationships. Maintaining face is important in Chinese social relations because face translates into power and influence and affects goodwill. It is critical to avoid losing face or causing the loss of face at all times.

In the Chinese culture in general, and to Chinese businessmen in particular, the concept of *face* is critical. *Face* refers both to the confidence of society in a person's moral character, as well as social perceptions of a person's prestige. Maintaining face is important in Chinese social relations because face translates into power and influence and affects goodwill. By extension, visual and descriptive images are of utmost importance in describing and presenting a business in its business plan.[2]

Because of the *importance of face*, the typical Chinese business plan is very short on financial information and very long on vague and general

---

[1] For your convenience, Chapter 10 contains a summary of all fifteen Refkin's Rules for conducting business in China.

[2] For an excellent and comprehensive review of Chinese language, culture, customs, and etiquette, please visit Kwintessential Cross Cultural Solutions at http://www.kwintessential.co.uk/resources/global-etiquette /china-country-profile.html. This web site was accessed on May 1, 2011.

descriptions of the company and the "big boss." In terms of financial information, Chinese business plans often project revenues and earnings doubling or tripling during the next five years without providing any substantiating support or evidence whatsoever for those assumptions. In contrast, most Western business plans clearly state critical assumptions, facts, and figures to support projections and expectations. Financial descriptions and projections are the most important components of a Western plan. Balance sheets, income statements, and cash flow statements provide Western businessmen with the image they are looking for to assess the health of a company. This is *not* generally the case for Chinese company business plans.

To illustrate, I once received a business plan from a Chinese company that manufactured environmental equipment for large industrial companies. When the firm's CEO handed me his company's business plan, I was both surprised and confused to see a large glossy photo of a Chinese fighter jet firing a missile on the plan's cover. (Figure 1 contains a copy of the actual photo pictured on the cover.) I wondered how either the jet or the missile could possibly be relevant to the business of an environmental equipment manufacturer. It took only a few questions and a little prodding to find the answer. The jet and the missile had absolutely nothing to do with the business! When I then asked the CEO why he would include a photo of a Chinese fighter jet firing a missile on the cover of his business plan, he told me he did so because he thought it would make his company appear more exciting and powerful than if he printed a photo of his company's blocky-looking products. To the CEO, the business plan was all about image and impression. Jets and missiles had nothing whatsoever to do with his company or its products. And plans like this one are the rule, not the exception, in China.

FIGURE 1

PHOTO ON COVER OF AN ENVIRONMENTAL EQUIPMENT MANUFACTURER'S BUSINESS PLAN

In general, I have found that it is very difficult to determine what a Chinese company produces, let alone how it performs, simply by reading its business plan. Chinese business plans emphasize the strength, achievement, and greatness of the company's leaders and employ bold and grandiose language and statements focusing on how the company will dominate and conquer all potential competition. Financial facts, figures, and projections are often missing. When financials are included, values are vague, undocumented, or just plain inaccurate.

As a result, when a Chinese firm hires me to assist them in raising Western capital, I spend a lot of my time and effort working with the company's finance and accounting departments to create focused business plans and to produce accurate historical and projected financial statements. This is no simple task. After my many years of experience working with dozens of Chinese firms, I can recall only one instance in which a firm's accounting and reporting system and financial statements did not require significant adjustment. In general, assets, revenues, and profits all are understated; the reason is simple and singular. Chinese businessmen (like businessmen around the world) don't want to pay taxes, and they use any means—both legal and illegal—to minimize their tax liability. The difference between the practice of tax avoidance by Chinese businessmen and their Western counterparts, however, is in terms of scale. In China very few companies pay the taxes they owe; in the United States relatively few companies evade taxes. Although China's government is largely aware that firms under its jurisdiction are evading taxes, it is often willing to turn a blind eye as long as the company continues to grow, provides increasing employment opportunities, and provides favors to important government VIPs.

For example, some time ago, a high-ranking government official referred me to a large auto parts manufacturer several hours outside of Shanghai that was experiencing meteoric growth. My first visit to the company convinced me that it had the potential to become listed on the NYSE in the near future. I was excited. After my visit, I called a good friend of mine, John Markum, who manages a large hedge fund that makes strategic investments in select Chinese companies prior to going public. John is a chartered financial analyst (CFA) and one of the smartest fund managers in the business.[3] I told John about the company, and I invited him to visit it with me on his next trip to China. Several weeks later, after touring the company and speaking with the local government officials (who pledged their full support for the company and its intention of going public in the United States), John shared my enthusiasm.

After he returned to the United States, John shared the company's business plan, which included current and projected financial statements, with his friend Dave, who was an investment banker at a major US financial institution. Based on that information, Dave gave John a verbal commitment—subject to the performance of standard due diligence that included a GAAP audit—to take the company public on US capital

---

[3]   The chartered financial analyst (CFA) designation is professional designation for finance and investment professionals working in investment management, investment banking, and other finance and investment related professions. For more information, see the CFA Institute at www.cfainstitute.org. This website was accessed on May 1, 2011.

markets. [4] Soon after conveying the good news to the owner of the Chinese firm, we received a pleasant surprise when the owner told us that one of his major suppliers committed to invest nearly $20 million into the transaction. Several days later, the parties signed a letter of intent and began the process by hiring an auditor to ensure they wasted no time.

They very much wanted to fast-track this transaction. And why wouldn't they? They had identified a solid Chinese company in a rapidly expanding industry that was experiencing meteoric growth; they had an outside Chinese investor that was willing to invest $20 million on the same terms as other investors, and the transaction had the full support and blessing of the Chinese government. What could go wrong?

It turns out—everything!

Almost as soon as auditors began poring over the company's books, they told us that we had major problems. First, the auditors informed us that the company hadn't paid most of its federal or local income taxes since 1999 (it was then 2007); they told us that the firm's annual revenue was barely half as much as had been reported to us (the owner of the company later told us that he destroyed the sales invoices as soon as money was collected to erase all paper trails and that his firm didn't recognize all of the revenues collected from customers); they informed us that the owner ran the company's revenue through his personal bank accounts and that he had switched these so often that it was impossible to piece together a paper trail to determine how much the company really earned. Of course the owner had done all of this to evade taxes, and everyone, including all of the government officials, knew it. None of them cared, of course, because this guy was the provincial model of success and employed thousands of workers.

---

[4]   Generally accepted accounting principles (GAAP) is the standard framework of guidelines for financial accounting. It includes the standards, conventions, and rules that accountants follow in recording and summarizing transactions and in the preparation of financial statements. For more information, see the Federal Accounting Standards Advisory Board (FASAB) at http://www .fasab.gov/accepted.html. This website was accessed on May 1, 2011.

Just when we were about to throw in the towel and walk away from the investment, our Chinese "partners" told us that a solution had suddenly materialized. First, we were approached by top local government officials who provided us with documents indicating that all local income tax liabilities were forgiven. Just like that! The federal tax liabilities (VAT taxes) were another story, however. We were told that we weren't likely to get a tax forgiveness letter from the national government (any more than we would expect to receive one from the IRS). Nevertheless, the local government's desire to help made us take a second look. And despite the lack of a financial paper trail, we understood enough about the company's business to know that it made a significant amount of money. Unfortunately, without supporting financial documentation, we couldn't pass a GAAP audit, and the company wouldn't be able to go public. The auditors simply did not have sufficient supporting documentation to create an auditable set of books.

Astonishingly, the very next day the company suddenly produced a complete set of auditable books along with all the necessary supporting documentation. "Mr. Alan, we are in luck! Look what we found!" the CFO exclaimed when he saw me. It became obvious to me then that neither the owner nor the government would give us any more information than they had to—but that successfully moving forward with the transaction and taking the company public was their most important objective—and the reason is obvious. Obtaining funding would enable the company to quickly expand and make more money; without it, they would be seriously constrained. Of course, the government was operating behind the scenes during the entire process. For government officials, the deal meant jobs for workers, kickbacks from the company, and enhanced political power. In addition, the government hoped to use this deal to attract additional foreign investors to their region that would provide even more capital to finance more deals. It was a massive moneymaking machine. I learned later that virtually all cities have offices dedicated to just this purpose. The fact that this small city was able to bring in $25 million in foreign capital meant a promotion (as we later found out) and increased prestige for the government officials. They weren't about to let this opportunity slip through their fingers.

While this series of events might seem unusual, I assure you it is not. Very few if any Chinese business owners will provide Western partners or investment bankers with any real financial figures unless they absolutely have to in order to get a deal done.

Figure 2 contains the financial projections I received from one Chinese firm (we'll call them China Inc.) that sought our assistance in securing outside funding. China Inc. provided no historical financial statements, budgets, spreadsheets, or assumptions to support their projections. They only provided what you see here.

Figure 2

Business/Investment Plan for China Inc.

- Projected revenue for 2006 is RMB 280 million ($38.36 million).
- Projected revenue for 2007 is RMB 400 million ($54.8 million).
- The required initial investment is 400 million RMB ($54.8 million).
- We plan to raise a total of RMB 3 billion ($410 million) during the first year.
- All construction work will be completed within 8 to 12 months.
- The existing workshop only took 6 months to complete.
- We plan to add two more production lines for manufacturing 100,000 cars.
- If we can raise RMB 100 million ($13.7 million) by the end of this year, our revenue will reach to RMB 2.2 billion ($300 million) in 2009.
- Distribution advantage: We have 760 auto parts sales agents throughout China, and we have 56 international sales agents in 22 different countries.

This sheet of paper they handed me basically said that if I helped them raise the $55 million initial investment, they would produce revenue of $410 million the year following completion of the project. That's it! That's all we got from a company that was (purportedly) generating annual revenue of $55 million a year right now. Believe it or not, this sort of financial forecast is what I typically receive from most mid-tier Chinese companies.

As another example, take a look at the excerpts from a business plan I received from another company (let's call it Mystery Inc.). Keep in mind that this plan has been edited grammatically to make it understandable. After reading it, see if you can guess what sort of business it is.

Figure 3

Business Plan for Mystery Inc.

I. **Overview**

Mystery Inc. was established on December 14, 2006 and is located in Beijing with an area about 250 square meters. Mystery Inc. currently has 18 employees, and 5 departments including the R&D Department, the Product Department, the UE Department, the Testing Department, and the Administration Department. Mystery Inc. has a management team comprised of a team manager, a project manager, ten researchers & developers, two product designers, two engineers, one tester, and one administrator.

Educational background of current employees

	Doctor	Master	Bachelor	Junior college
number	1	2	13	2
percentage	5%	11%	73%	11%

II. Present Status:

After six months of hard work, the initial edition of the website and the desktop-end beta version have been completed. The website primarily consists of a task system and a space system. The main purpose of the task system is to assign research tasks and participant tasks. The main purpose of the space system is to provide a space for users to display information about themselves. It also helps businesses understand participants and increases the retention of users.

Many of the main functions of the website such as text transfer capabilities, document transfer capabilities, and file management capabilities have largely been completed.

At present, our team has already set the product development plan for next phase, and we are expanding the scale of our group.

III. Product and Service

A. WEB Product (existing product)

As of July 31, 2007, we have finished the website beta version. Its functions include its information publishing system and its space system. In addition, we have already finished the development of a server end program which is based on distributed technology and has already passed the pressure test.

Information publishing systems include: task publication, task search, task settlement, and relevant supporting systems. We can operate the entire _____ business and provide formal _____ services.

The beta version provides users with an entire space to display and interact and includes a display center, an album, and individual file centers.

B. Vertical Searching Product (planned product)

A vertical searching product will be introduced into our platform by WEB Version 2. Version 2 will improve our product based on our searching technique and will increase the data capabilities of the website. This planned system will provide users with more convenient and comprehensive web search capabilities.

C. Desktop Software Product (existing product)

As of July 31, 2007 the development of desktop-end beta version has been completed. The desktop beta version is capable of providing text communications, document transmission, basic document transmission management, and other functions. Currently, over 30,000 customers have registered for the desktop-end software. We are further optimizing the desktop software program and are preparing it for testing.

D. The Combination of Desktop-end Software and WEB Product (under development)

The desktop beta version under development will provide a WEB link interface feature so that users' own information center can be directly opened by desktop-end software. Desktop-end software can also check other users' display centers. We plan to add custom-tailored information delivery, desktop-end information publication, and information retrieval systems in the next version of the desktop software.

E. Corporation Associated Products & Planning Products

Based on existing desktop-end software, we plan to add corporation associated elements to the desktop-end software during the next 6 months. Its service includes: document transmission, document transmission management, document sharing, document transfer, network hard disk, user rights setup. We will continue to optimize our products, and become the first-class _____ provider in China.

From your reading of this business plan, were you able to guess what this company was about? Did this plan help you to understand this company's business goals, it objectives, and its financial potential? Not likely.

Believe it or not, this plan was for a company that was to be a spin-off of a larger company that was generating huge annual revenue and was extremely profitable. Unfortunately, the firm's management could not effectively communicate and therefore failed in their attempts to develop a business relationship with banks and other financial institutions outside of China.

The fact is, managers at Chinese firms that I've been associated with are not very good at writing comprehensive business plans, developing realistic financial projections, or marketing their firm's potential. While I have seen a few instances of well thought-out business plans with good financial projections from Chinese companies, it's simply not common. The poor quality reflected in the business plan produced by Mystery Inc. is not the exception in China—it's the rule. As a result, I spend a great deal of my time helping my Chinese clients restructure their business and financial goals into a coherent business plan that will serve as a road map for the future. While that task hasn't been easy, once we've accomplished it, the path to success has been much easier.

The following day I spoke to my friends at ABC Capital. Like me, the folks at ABC were astonished that the Chinese company had agreed to pay for our trip. The real challenge this exciting opportunity presented for the people at ABC, however, was to clear enough time on their calendars to make the trip. I knew from experience that it was no easy task for a solid US company to get an hour meeting with ABC Capital. Here I was asking them to give up an entire week for a company in China that they knew nothing about!

Tom Jones was my close friend and a managing partner at ABC Capital. Tom told me to give him a day, and he'd see if he could rearrange his calendar to accommodate the trip. The next day he called back and told me that he'd been able to clear his overflowing calendar for a week during the following month. He told me that he'd use this time to visit a client in Australia, a trip he'd been putting off for a while, and then spend three days in Beijing. The plan was for me to get there ahead of him and gather the information he needed for his visit. Ken would also accompany us to Beijing. Since Ken was acquainted with the owners of the company we were going to look at and also spoke fluent Mandarin, he'd act both as our business associate and as interpreter during our visit. The three of us coordinated our calendars during the day and set a firm date for our departure, and Ken helped us process the paperwork for our business visas.

If I was surprised that I was actually going to do this—that I was actually traveling to China and considering doing business there—my wife Debbie was even more surprised about our upcoming trip. I told her that although I hadn't actually expected to make this trip when I started talking about it over coffee with Ken, I was now locked into it. The trip was set. I told my wife that she didn't have to go and that if she wanted to back out I would explain it to the Chinese, and she could stay in Florida, which was about forty degrees warmer than Beijing during the time we would be there in November.

My wife has always been a good trooper about traveling around the world with me. Also, since she is my business partner, she was also very interested in the business aspect of the trip. In many ways she adapted a lot better than I did to some of the exotic locations we traveled to. In the end, this trip to China proved to be no exception. She said she was excited about the business, shopping, touring the Great Wall, and visiting other attractions that this ancient and culturally rich country could offer. Looking back now, I think my wife said this more out of support for me rather than for her sense of adventure. In fact, at the time we were right in the middle of building a new house in Florida, and I knew she was up to her neck every day in dealing with the contractors and in selecting the hundreds of materials and finishes that go into building a custom house. The contractor never came to me to make a decision; he knew that my wife held the throne in that regard.

CHAPTER 2 ══════════

First Trip to China

Finally the day of our departure came. As promised, our Chinese hosts purchased business class tickets for everyone in our party—me, my wife, my friend Tom from ABC Capital, and Dennis, who worked with Tom. However, to get us the cheapest business class seats available, they arranged a less than direct route, connecting through both Detroit and Narita, Japan, on our way to Beijing. The flight was generally uneventful, and we arrived in the early evening.

Despite the twelve-hour time difference between Florida and China, we all felt pretty good. The jet lag we expected hadn't set in, and Beijing Capital Airport wasn't as busy as we had heard it would be. I also noticed how remarkable it was that all of the workers at the airport—without exception—were extremely polite and helpful. And most were very young. In fact, it didn't look like anyone working at the terminal was over thirty. The entire workforce looked bright and well trained for their jobs. It made a notable first impression on all of us.

As we were being processed through the airport, I was surprised at how much faster going through Chinese customs and immigration was than in the United States. There were at least two dozen booths available to accommodate the hundreds of international travelers who had arrived along with us on that day; it took us fifteen minutes at most. After clearing China customs and immigration, we walked toward the exit and handed the immigration officer our immigration card. He waved us by with barely a glance, and we emerged through a set of large glass doors into the international arrivals concourse at the old Beijing Capital International Airport.

I've been through a great many international arrival concourses during my travels, but none matched the pandemonium that greeted my wife and me on our arrival in Beijing. There was a solid wall of people standing in front of us, all waving and trying to get the attention of someone entering the main terminal. There were also scores of baggage handlers, taxi drivers, and hotel representatives, all contributing to the chaos.

In the midst of this turmoil Ken ran up to an overweight man in his late fifties who was with a woman I assumed was his wife. Ken was the only one of our party who spoke Chinese, knew the details of our arrangements, and had met the owner of the company we were here to meet with, so I assumed this was his contact, Mr. Wong. They embraced and spoke to each other briefly in Chinese. A few seconds later the three of them walked over to us, and Ken introduced us to Mr. and Mrs. Wong, the owners of AutoStar. Standing behind Mr. and Mrs. Wong was a large group of people, all impeccably dressed, and all smiling and waving at us. Then, as if they'd done so hundreds of times, two of that group—both women—happily handed my wife and me beautiful bouquets of flowers.

I barely had a chance to thank them before several uniformed drivers came forward, grabbed our luggage, and plowed through the turbulent crowd straight out of the terminal. Exiting the terminal and holding the bouquets, we walked outside to find the drivers waiting with the doors open to brand new Mercedes and Audis. I was amazed!

Before I knew what was happening, we were in our cars and weaving in and out of traffic on the Beijing airport expressway. Because of the distance and stop-and-go traffic (which is the rule in Beijing, not the exception, I was told), and despite our drivers' best efforts, it took us more than an hour to go from the airport in the northeast part of the city to our hotel on the west side of Beijing. For those of you who haven't been to Beijing before, the east side of the city is where most of the foreign embassies, main business districts, international restaurants, and higher-end hotels tend to be located. It's the upscale part of Beijing. The west side—where we were staying—was the Chinese business district, and it was where AutoStar's business offices were located. During the long ride into the city, our hosts made sure we drove past Beijing's most famous landmarks: the Forbidden City, the Temple of Heaven, the People's Congress, and

Tiananmen Square. Throughout our drive the entire city was beautifully lit up and sparkled as the sun went down. It made an indelible impression on all of us.

Before the trip, I had often heard that Beijing was an immense city. I had lived in Los Angeles in the past, so I was used to *big*. Still, I was completely unprepared for the sheer density of buildings and humanity as we dodged traffic on the way to the hotel. With the cool of riverboat gamblers, our drivers would suddenly dart across five lanes of Beijing rush-hour traffic, weaving in and out while honking their horns and cutting off pedestrians, bicyclists, and other cars. On that first trip alone, we witnessed our drivers speed along the shoulder of the freeway, cut off police cars, and squeeze down bicycle paths in order to speed us to our destination. Now if it was just our drivers driving this way that would be one thing. But the fact is that virtually everyone who drives a car in China drives the same way. Call it Rome on steroids. Traffic lanes, stop signs, and streetlights are more like suggestions rather than rules to be followed or enforced. Our driver, Wong Wei, whom we affectionately called "Wrong Way" (a nickname that has stuck with him to this day), never broke a sweat as he drove like this through the heart of Beijing.

As we pulled in front of our hotel, I was a bit surprised to see Mr. and Mrs. Wong and their entourage (composed primarily of Mr. and Mrs. Wong's children) already waiting there for us—smiling and waving just as they had been at the airport. Apparently they had instructed our drivers to take a more indirect route to allow us to see many of Beijing's most famous landmarks.

After being greeted again by our new associates and registering at the front desk, we were handed our room keys and were told that our luggage was already waiting for us in our rooms. I was very impressed by this demonstration of hospitality—the degree to which I had rarely seen during my extensive international travel experience as a corporate VIP. Our Chinese hotel was opulent and elegant, even by Western standards. All of the hotel service personnel—from the front desk clerks to the concierge—were dressed impeccably and spoke fluent English with just a touch of accent. Our rooms were very clean, comfortable, and well appointed. Overall, my initial impressions of China and the Chinese people were overwhelmingly positive—and those feelings grew stronger as time passed.

Later that first evening, after relaxing and freshening up, our hosts treated us to what I was told was a traditional Chinese business banquet—an extremely important event in the Chinese culture. For those of you reading this that have never traveled to China on business, understanding the importance of the Chinese business dinner cannot be overemphasized. That first evening, our hosts took us to Beijing's famous Da Zhai Men Restaurant, a fabulous eighteenth-century-themed Qing Dynasty destination. Da Zhai Men had the appearance of one of Beijing's hutongs—traditional courtyard residences that regularly span several city blocks. As we walked through the front gate, we were greeted by an army of waiters and waitresses, all attired in traditional Qing Dynasty Chinese silk. Each of the small residences within the hutong contained from one to several private rooms within which groups of diners were seated—usually at enormous circular tables with a lazy Susan in the center upon which the main entrees were placed. As we were led through several winding and beautifully landscaped courtyards by an elegant, young, English-speaking hostess, we were serenaded by musicians, magicians, and other entertainers. Wow! This was really something!

We finally arrived at our dining residence within the hutong, which contained only one room with an enormous circular table in the middle—large enough to seat our entire twelve-person party. It was clear that this particular building within the complex was more secluded and seemed to offer an exceptional degree of privacy. The choice of this location was clearly meant by our hosts to convey importance.

When it came time to sit, it quickly became apparent that the seating arrangement also was very important. I was asked to sit in the "seat of honor"—which was the chair most directly facing the door to the building. I was politely taught that this seat is often designated by a napkin that is folded in a different manner compared to the others on the table—usually artistically inserted into an empty water glass. Also according to Beijing tradition, my host, Mr. Wong, was seated opposite of me—so that we directly faced each other during the entire meal. The Chinese generally prefer the use of a circular table at business banquets so that everyone in the party can see and speak to each without leaning forward or turning our bodies or heads. My wife was seated next to me, and Mr. Wong's wife was seated next to him. The rest of the party was seated relative to the host and guest of honor more or less in order of importance and to facilitate language interpretation.

At that moment, I turned to look at my wife and could tell from the expression on her face that she was thinking the same thing I was. What in the world were we having for dinner!? We had both heard the stories that the Chinese eat just about anything—from snakes to scorpions to turtle brain soup.

A moment later our host asked us if we preferred beer or wine to accompany our dinner. I learned from Ken (who was now sitting next to me on my left) on the plane trip over to China that my choice would likely determine what everyone would drink that evening. Ken also told me that most beverages in China, including beer, generally are served warm. Knowing this and knowing my wife's preference for white wine, I quickly said that I would prefer white wine. What a mistake THAT turned out to be! When I ordered the white wine, I was picturing a nice chardonnay or Fume Blanc in a bucket of ice. What we got was VERY different! A few moments later, one of our four stunningly beautiful servers brought out a small, delicate bottle of a clear liquid, which she carefully poured into small short-stemmed glasses the size of shot glasses. Next to me, I heard Ken let out a muffled sigh that suggested a degree of discomfort. He then explained to my wife and me that this was baijiu (pronounced "by joe"), or what we might call grain alcohol, moonshine, or white lightning in the States.

At that point, Mr. Wong commanded our table's attention. He stood up and lectured that China has many different types and brands of baijiu, which vary in terms of alcohol content, taste, and color. The baijiu being served that night, our host proudly boasted, was China's very best and most famous brand! I later learned that in China the quality of baijiu is often measured by alcohol content and that the baijiu we drank was 60% alcohol or 120 proof! Of course, at the time we had no way of knowing this—and that had been their intent! As Mr. Wong and our other hosts rose from their seats and offered us a toast welcoming us to Beijing, I noticed that they watched us intently as they roared in unison, *"ganbei!"*, or "bottoms up," in Chinese. As I threw my head back and drank the clear, watery-looking liquid in a single gulp, my throat immediately seemed on fire and tears welled in my eyes. I looked across at my wife, Ken, Tom, and Dennis, who also choked down the potent, fiery liquid to the delight of the clapping Chinese. After that first toast we sat down, and Ken told us that tradition demanded that we soon follow our hosts with a similar toast. Shortly after, I proposed a toast, thanking our hosts for their hospitality and wishing us all mutual success. After my toast was interpreted, the entire party stood up and in unison shouted *"ganbei!"* before we placed our glasses near our lips. As we sat down to eat, Ken turned to me and whispered that he thought dinner already was going very, very well.

After this initial round of toasts, all of the men in the Wong party simultaneously pulled out packs of cigarettes, offering the particular brand they favored to each other and to us. To our astonishment, and right at the beginning of dinner, they all lit up! Smoking, it seems, is another Chinese business tradition. In China, I later learned, nearly 70% of adult men smoke cigarettes.

As the night wore on, it quickly became apparent that drinking and smoking were an integral part of Chinese business banquets. This is particularly true—I was to learn later—when meeting with government officials. It seems that it's almost a requirement to have the proverbial "hollow leg" if you want to go into government service in China. I can't count the number of times I turned down a drink at a business dinner gathering—only to have a government official fill my glass and grinningly bellow *"ganbei!"*

At virtually every business dinner or meeting I've had in China over the ensuing years—and there have been scores—I've refused a cigarette when it's been offered, only to have my host flick his lighter with one hand and give me the cigarette in the other. After years of these refusals, I've found that it's simply easier to drink and light up (although I smoke cigars, and smoke the cigarette given to me the same way) rather than to turn down the offers. There's no doubt that when both sides to a business transaction in China socialize—dine, drink, and smoke—together, it is easier to develop closer and more mutually trusting friendships and business relationships.

After our initial round of toasts and the many more that followed, several courses of vegetables, meats, dumplings, and pastries were brought out in large serving bowls and platters and placed on the large lazy Susan. Mr. Wong was consistent and deliberate in making sure each new addition to our feast that was placed on the turnstile was first presented to me. The main course on this evening was Beijing's famous *Peking duck*, which is served with thinly sliced scallions and black bean sauce rolled into thin and flat pita-like bread. The main courses were followed at the end with desserts consisting of both assorted sweet pastries and all varieties of fresh fruit, including apples, watermelon, pineapple, grapes, and peaches. In all, the entire experience was not only wonderfully divine, but it also served as an important icebreaker in helping participants from both sides get to know one another before beginning the long negotiation process in the days to come. As I came to know later on, the dinner mainly served as a way to fatten up the livestock before moving in for the kill. This brings me to Refkin's Rule #2.

> **Refkin's Rule #2: At dinner, always remember that you're the "main course."** In China, business banquets and dinners are an extremely important part of the business process. The most important thing for foreign businessmen to understand about these events is that they are always the "main course."

As is customary, our host, Mr. Wong, subtly signaled when it was time to depart. We all arose, thanked our host for his wonderful hospitality, and were shepherded to our awaiting cars. We arrived at our hotel with the promise that they would pick us up at the hotel at nine o'clock the following morning to begin business discussions.

The next morning, after breakfast at the hotel, our Chinese hosts picked us up exactly at nine. During my time in China over the years, I've found that Chinese businessmen and government officials are very prompt and detail-oriented; nothing is spontaneous or left to chance, and they plan meticulously. As we walked into the lobby we were met by our host. Mr. Wong warmly greeted us and introduced us to Maria, a recent graduate of a good university in southern China that he hired to act as an interpreter for my wife and the other women in his family. Ken would continue to interpret for me in our business meetings with Mr. Wong and his associates. Although women in China are now more equal and enjoy far greater opportunity than they did thirty years ago, China still is largely a man's world. Accordingly, our host had planned an entire day of shopping and sightseeing for my wife while the rest of us—all men—attended to business.

As we all stepped out of the hotel lobby and onto the carport, we saw a caravan of three gleaming, new, black luxury cars lined up with their doors open and attendants at hand, waiting for us to enter like arriving dignitaries. We got into our cars, and after a short drive we arrived at AutoStar's offices—located in a forty-story office building near the center of the city. We were ushered into an elegant atrium and then were directed to a large conference room, where the other members of Mr. Wong's family were patiently waiting for us. In preparation for our negotiations, I was again seated directly across from Mr. Wong. This time, however, negotiations were conducted at a massive rectangular cherry wood conference table, not unlike those typically employed in conference rooms in businesses in the United States. Mr. Wong's team sat on either side of him while Tom, Dennis, and Ken surrounded me. The atmosphere on this morning couldn't have been more different from dinner the evening before. Today the smiles were gone, and expressions were suddenly much more serious. The atmosphere was decidedly more competitive—more confrontational.

The mood softened just a bit when Mr. Wong began the meeting by warmly welcoming us and thanking us for making this long trip to see him and his family and to learn more about his company. He then said that he would begin our discussions by showing us a PowerPoint presentation that would provide a comprehensive overview of AutoStar, which included its past development and future plans.

With that, our host dimmed the lights and made a very professional presentation—even by US standards. According to Mr. Wong, AutoStar operated automotive repair centers in locations throughout Beijing, and was one of the largest chains of automotive repair service providers in

Beijing. With adequate financing, Mr. Wong asserted that AutoStar could become the largest auto repair and service company in China. Operating activities at these centers included the painting and repair of automobiles; sales of automotive parts, accessories, and supplies; and the sale of automotive insurance.

According to Mr. Wong, at the time there were about 2.3 million vehicles in the city of Beijing, a metropolis with a population of about fourteen million people—a number that is expected to double by the year 2020. Rapid urbanization along with a breathtaking expansion of private automobile ownership would result in an explosive escalation in the demand for higher-quality automotive maintenance services. According to Mr. Wong, AutoStar was perfectly positioned to provide automotive services with the quality and volume capabilities necessary to meet this rapidly increasing demand for these services.

Financially, the presentation showed that AutoStar generated RMB 80 million (about US $11 million at the time) in annual revenue in 2004. Asset growth also was expanding significantly.[5] According to Mr. Wong, with the addition of just a little outside capital, the growth of the company would more than double during the first year through the addition of new service stores in the Beijing area. After that, the company would continue to grow exponentially both inside Beijing and beyond as it expanded geographically and added additional stores. Mr. Wong patiently explained that he possessed a powerful, valuable, and unique competitive

---

[5] RMB is an abbreviation for renminbi. Renminbi literally means "people's currency." Renminbi is also often referred to as "yuan" and is the official currency in the mainland of the People's Republic of China (PRC). It is issued by the People's Bank of China, the monetary authority of the PRC. The official abbreviation is CNY (for Chinese yuan), although also commonly abbreviated as "RMB." The Latinized symbol is ¥ . In recent years, the RMB has been strengthening against the US dollar. The exchange rate between the US dollar and renminbi was RMB 7.1058 = $1 on March 1, 2008. For further discussion and references about the renminbi, see its Wikipedia profile at http://en.wikipedia.org/wiki/Renminbi. This page was accessed May 1, 2011.

advantage—Chinese government contracts that he acquired through his considerable personal relationships built after many years in government service. Unfortunately, said Mr. Wong, he could not fully capitalize on those contracts and was, in fact, turning away business because he was not able to expand and accommodate this additional business.[6]

As Mr. Wong finished his presentation, all of us on our team furtively glanced at one another. Through eye contact, we all agreed that we were impressed and interested in learning more. However, although I've never worked in China, I had been doing this sort of business for several decades and have been pitched to by the best of them. So at this point we began to ask the sorts of questions that we always do at first meetings such as this one. "How many employees do you have at each location?" "How much does it cost to build a new store?" "Who is your main competition?" "Do you keep an accurate set of books that we could see?" As we asked, without exception, Mr. Wong and his team provided positive and detailed response. We thought we were asking the right questions and getting solid answers. Our Chinese hosts seemed quite knowledgeable, and in the rare cases in which they did not have a ready answer, they happily agreed to do anything we asked and provide any additional information we needed.[7]

---

[6]   This is a statement I often hear to this day. Many of the companies I see in China are hampered by a lack of access to capital. Since the banks in China are asset-based lenders and do not give term loans or revolvers, many companies have their growth thwarted by a lack of expansion capital while their business opportunities continue to abound. I've experienced many companies that could almost overnight double their revenue and increase their earnings if they could add production lines and buy additional materials. That's one of the many reasons they seek and need foreign capital.

[7]   Looking back on that first day years later, it was clear that I assumed the company was telling the truth and that the documentation I and ABC Capital received was factually correct or at least close to it. I was looking at this opportunity through rose-colored glasses and didn't understand the culture and traditions of China. I was new to China and had no experience whatsoever doing business with the Chinese. Now that I am scarred, seasoned, and China savvy, I don't make the same assumptions that I did back then.

When it came time to talk money, our host was well prepared. I asked Mr. Wong how much money AutoStar needed to execute its business plan, and he responded without the slightest hesitation that AutoStar needed $8 million in funding. The certainty and specificity of his response momentarily caught me off guard. This was a question he had obviously anticipated and was prepared to respond to. He was not in the least bit shy about asking us for the $8 million. At that point, those of us at the table turned slightly toward Tom to hear what he had to say. Tom was emotionless in his reaction, saying only that ABC Capital would study the information provided to us as well as the additional data we had requested and would respond to AutoStar sometime after we returned home. With that said, our first meeting ended.

Mr. Wong assigned his nephew and assistant, Mr. Li, to accompany us and act as a personal assistant during our visit. Mr. Li was a good-natured, short, slightly overweight, middle-aged fellow who always seemed to have a smile on his face. Because Mr. Wong placed so much importance on us and on our visit, Mr. Li stuck to us like glue to ensure that our visit was perfectly choreographed—cars, lunches, dinners, tours—everything. I had a strong sense that if something went wrong during Mr. Li's watch, Mr. Wong would have his head!

That evening, Mr. Wong again arranged a fabulous banquet for us at another famous Beijing restaurant. This second dinner was a bit more relaxed than the first, now that we knew our potential partners better after completing a somewhat stressful day of business negotiations.

My wife told me that she had a great time touring Beijing during the day while we were at our meeting. She said she went to the Forbidden City in the morning, had a fabulous lunch at an upscale downtown restaurant, and finished her day with an afternoon shopping spree accompanied by several of the female members of the Wong family. Although she seemed a bit fatigued from all of the activities that day, I could tell my wife really was enjoying the first-class treatment we all were receiving. When dinner was over, we were ushered back to our hotel, exhausted from the combination of jet lag, great food, and nonstop activity.

The following day, while my wife was again shopping and sightseeing, Mr. Wong took our team on a tour of one of AutoStar's service centers. The shop in the main building, which I estimated occupied about twenty thousand square feet of floor space, was buzzing with activity. Technicians were busy servicing cars in one of AutoStar's eight auto bays while clerks and service personnel were busy servicing customers. In addition to the service bays, Mr. Wong paused and pointed to two large bake ovens, which he said were used specifically for painting cars.[8] We also toured an upstairs area that seemed to serve as a cross between an AutoStar museum and auto parts store. The walls contained scores of framed photos of Mr. Wong and his family, while the floor space was stocked full of cleaning and polishing products, apparel, and other kinds of auto accessories.

After finishing our tour of the main building, Mr. Wong took us next door to AutoStar's second building at that location. Mr. Wong explained that this building, which was quiet compared to the main facility, was reserved for those working only on government vehicles, which AutoStar had a special contract for through his personal connections and many years of service with the central government.[9]

During the afternoon, our host took us on a brief tour around Beijing. The scale of China's capital city was hard to fathom. As a person who lived in Los Angeles for much of my life, I was used to living and working in large cities. Still, even Los Angeles doesn't hold a candle to Beijing in terms of

---

[8]   We learned much later that—contrary to what AutoStar told us—the bake ovens were not bake ovens at all. They were merely enclosures they used for painting cars. We also later found out, through an employee that we became friends with who left the company, that the cars we saw during our tour that day did not belong to customers but instead belonged to management staff and friends who, knowing the time of our arrival, drove them into the facility, creating the appearance of cars, cars, everywhere.

[9]   We later discovered that this building did not belong to AutoStar at all and that they had no responsibility whatsoever for any of the cars in that building we saw that day. To the workers in that building, we were just a group of Americans who walked through their facility accompanied by a well-dressed and important Chinese guy.

the number and concentration of people, buildings, and businesses. And the pace of construction of relatively fast-growing south Florida didn't remotely compare to the hundreds of cranes perched atop a seemingly infinite sea of skyscrapers and high-rises dotting the Beijing skyline.[10]

When we got back to the hotel after the tour, Ken, Tom, Dennis, and I met briefly in the lobby to discuss what we had seen and experienced during the past two days. We all agreed we were impressed by Mr. Wong, as well as by the apparent opportunity AutoStar offered as an investment in China's obviously fast-growing auto services market in the most rapidly growing economy in the world.

Our third day in Beijing began much like the previous two. The plan was for my wife to go sightseeing and shopping with Mrs. Wong and the other female members of the Wong family while men met to discuss business. In the morning, we went back to AutoStar's headquarters and were led to a conference room to discuss the only thing that *really* matters in China—*money*! This brings me to Refkin's Rule #3.

> **Refkin's Rule #3: The Chinese always have a game plan, and the plan is always all about money.** The primary objective of Chinese businessmen who do business with foreign business partners is to extract as much money as possible as soon as possible. All other plans or objectives are simply icing on the cake. Chinese businessmen always have well thought-out and detailed game plans—and those plans always center on money.

I realize that Refkin's Rule #3 might seem overly simplistic for those of you reading this that have never done business in China. However, for Western businessmen that have navigated the treacherous minefields of business in modern capitalist China, we know there is absolutely nothing more important to Chinese businessmen. *It's always all about money.*

---

[10] The Florida real estate market was booming at the time of our first trip to China in 2005.

I've lost count of the number of Chinese companies I've consulted for during the past few years. Some of these firms have hired me to help them identify a Western joint venture investor and partner; some firms have sought my assistance in helping them to update their technology or production and management systems, and some firms have asked for help in improving and modernizing their accounting systems and financial controls. In the end, however, no matter what the initial reason for my meetings with Chinese firms might have been, the discussion eventually leads to the same thing—their desire for financing—money—*cash*! "So you need my help in assembling a joint venture?" I ask. "*Yes*!" they say. Chinese translation = *we want cash*! "So you need my help in exporting and distributing your products in the United States?" I ask. "*Yes*!" they exclaim. Chinese translation = *we want cash*! "You say your business is growing so rapidly that you need financing in order to take on and fill all of the new orders you're getting?" "*Yes*!" they exclaim. Chinese translation = *we want cash*! In other words, *it's always all about the money*.

Part of the reason for the single-minded focus on money is cultural. For example, if you go to a Chinese wedding, you don't even have to think about what you bring for a gift. In the United States, one normally purchases a present that will symbolically help to launch the young couple's life into the future: a beautiful painting to decorate the couple's new home, a set of fine china or dinnerware, a silver chafing dish. In China, you can forget all about that. Just bring the money. Simply tuck your contribution neatly away in a red envelope, drop it in a basket on your way in, and you're done. Dr. Borgia actually met and married his wife Jia in China and so has firsthand knowledge of the process. The two greatest measures of the success at a wedding are how much cash the couple receives at the reception and how large a dowry the groom's family pays to the bride's parents for the honor of marrying their daughter. If the value of these two sums isn't large enough, the bride and her family lose face and the entire event devolves into disaster.[11] Chinese New Year, or Spring Festival, also

---

[11] The actual wedding does not take place on the day of the reception. The wedding normally takes place at a government office in the provincial capital several days to a week before the wedding celebration. In Dr. Borgia's case, the actual marriage took place in the city of Shijiazhuang, the capital city of Hebei province, a week before his reception.

includes the gift of money in little red envelopes to attending children as a central theme of the event.[12] In China, money is the central focus in the lives of most people. It is a measure of a person's efforts, symbolizes intelligence and stature, and provides face. It is what most Chinese people strive for in life. Culturally speaking, everything else is window dressing.

During our meeting on that third day, Mr. Wong again explained that AutoStar needed $8 million to open new facilities and expand business to try and keep up with the ever-growing demand for automotive repair in China. To us, this request did not appear to be terribly unreasonable, assuming the validity of AutoStar's historical operating and financial performance information as well as the feasibility of the company's projected financial potential as outlined in the information package that we discussed. Tom told me his staff would have to go through the books and records and perform their own due diligence prior to making an investment, but that was standard prior to committing any funds. Our own brief personal experience in China on this trip seemed to support the growth projection assessment. The traffic in Beijing was far heavier than the traffic I had experienced while living in Los Angeles or Seattle, even though widespread automobile ownership by Chinese citizens was a relatively recent phenomenon! Incredible! All of this supported the idea that the demand for professional automotive services in Beijing and throughout China would continue to grow rapidly in the future.

---

[12] Chinese New Year, or Spring Festival, as it is also called, is the most important of all traditional Chinese holidays. This holiday also is known as the Lunar New Year. Chinese New Year traditionally begins on the first day of the first lunar month (Chinese: 正月; pinyin: zhēng yuè) in the Chinese calendar and ends fifteen days later; the last is a special part of the holiday called the Lantern Festival. During Spring Festival, individuals living and working away from their hometowns return home to celebrate the holiday with their family and friends, a practice known as "new-year visits" (Chinese: 正月; pinyin: bàinián). The color red is liberally used in all decorations, and little red envelopes containing money are given to children by their parents and grandparents. For further discussion of the Chinese New Year holidays, see its Wikipedia profile at http://en.wikipedia.org/wiki/Chinese_New_Year.

Prior to sitting down, Tom told me privately that he would seriously consider making AutoStar ABC Capital's initial investment in China. One obstacle that presented itself early, however, was that ABC Capital could invest only in publicly listed companies—or in companies that soon would become publicly listed. Since Mr. Wong's company was clearly private (and Chinese to boot!), AutoStar was not going to get funded by ABC Capital (or any other Western hedge fund, for that matter) unless Mr. Wong made a commitment to take AutoStar public on US capital markets—and to do so within a relatively short time frame. Obviously, this issue had to be resolved immediately before either side invested any more time or money in the relationship.

As we took our assigned seats at the conference table, Tom thanked Mr. Wong for the tour and told him that his fund was impressed with what he had seen—both of China in general and AutoStar in particular. However, Tom explained that it was his fund's policy only to invest money in public companies and that ABC Capital would not be able to provide capital unless Mr. Wong would quickly begin the process of preparing to take AutoStar public on US financial markets.

It was impossible from his expressionless face to know whether Mr. Wong was surprised to hear what Tom had just told him. Nevertheless, with a great deal of politeness and humility, Mr. Wong suddenly rose, excused himself, and without saying a word, he and his team silently left the conference room. After they left, I turned to Ken for an explanation, and he told Tom and me that Mr. Wong and his family were likely having a strategy meeting to decide how to respond to Tom's statements.[13] About thirty minutes later Mr. Wong and his team returned to the conference room and informed us that because obtaining capital to expand AutoStar was their most important objective, they would follow our advice and

---

[13] Today, after several years of doing business in China, I've learned that whenever a new or complex issue arises to confront a Chinese leader, the leader usually will close ranks and discuss the issue with his inner circle of friends and family members before providing any response. That's precisely what occurred in this case.

do whatever was necessary—including taking the company public. This brings me to Refkin's Rule #4:

> **Refkin's Rule #4: There is never an exception to Refkin's Rule #3 (The Chinese always have a game plan, and the plan is always all about the money).** No elaboration required.

As I would later come to learn, Mr. Wong (and virtually every other Chinese business leader I have met since then) would be willing to do or say whatever was necessary to get as much cash as possible as soon as possible. When doing business in China, it's always all about the money.

As far as Mr. Wong and his family were concerned, the issue had been decided. They would do what was necessary to take AutoStar public, and in return Tom and ABC Capital would help them to raise the $8 million in capital they needed to realize the company's potential. Mr. Wong emphasized that he would do whatever was necessary to achieve that objective. At that point, Mr. Wong proceeded to show us architectural renderings and floor plans for three different types of service facilities that AutoStar planned to construct once they received the funding. When Mr. Wong finished speaking, one of his sons immediately stood up and announced that AutoStar already had identified sixty new expansion sites it could lease throughout China and proceeded to show us a map of China (in English) with the target cities clearly identified. As his son spoke, Mr. Wong thumbed through a ledger book an inch thick—written in Chinese—which Ken verified, detailed the leases for these sixty sites just waiting for his signature.

As the meeting ended, Tom asked for additional specific background information and data, and told Mr. Wong that, for AutoStar to go public on US markets, as a prerequisite, he would have to pay for a GAAP (generally accepted accounting principles) audit by an internationally accredited accounting firm. Until that audit was performed, Tom explained, it would be impossible to move forward. Unimpressed, Mr. Wong adamantly promised to get us our audit right away. I knew by the immediacy of his response that Mr. Wong obviously had no comprehension whatsoever about what a GAAP audit meant.

After the meeting Mr. Li approached us and, with a bit of shyness, told us that Mr. Wong would like for the group to sign a letter of intent before concluding and departing back to the States. I was surprised and unprepared to be presented with such a request so soon! I was even more taken aback that this request was presented to me by Mr. Li, one of Mr. Wong's subordinates, rather than by the boss himself! This brings me to Refkin's Rule #5:

> **Refkin's Rule #5: The boss never approaches you directly. He almost always uses an intermediary.** When doing business with foreign partners, the "boss" (CEO/leader) on the Chinese side rarely approaches the foreign business leader directly. The boss almost always uses an intermediary for everything from initial contacts to negotiation to conveying news.

If you've ever read the book or seen the film *The Godfather*, you know that the Godfather only gives orders through a close circle of intermediaries, and he always leaves it to his subordinates to carry those orders out. This ensures that it would be very difficult for anyone to implicate the Godfather in violent or illegal activity. I've learned through my experience that Chinese families and businesses are organized in much the same way. Although Mr. Wong was the leader of the company and desired the letter of intent, he left the actual execution of the request to his nephew Mr. Li, to avoid losing face with Tom if he declined. Ever since that first time I've found that, without exception, the leader on the Chinese side rarely makes a request directly. The boss almost always uses an intermediary.

As an example, the uncle (we'll call him Zhou) of the CEO of a company I was consulting for asked me one weekend if I'd been to a local park in Beijing called Maple Mountain. It's a stunningly beautiful place where walking trails meander through statuesque maple trees, whose leaves turn a brilliant burnt red color during the fall of each year. Seasoned in the ways of doing business in China by then, I knew well Uncle Zhou's reason for asking me on the tour was not so that we could bond, but because he needed to talk to me in private. I knew that probably meant he had a difficult question or request or that he had bad news to convey.

About a half an hour into our walk, Uncle Zhou began to talk about how difficult it was for his nephew's firm to adapt to Western accounting systems and standards. He said that both he and his nephew were disappointed with members of the firm's accounting department because they had not performed as expected. When I asked him what sorts of errors the accounting department had made, he told me that the firm's revenues and profits for the current quarter would significantly miss the projections that I had been given just a couple of weeks earlier, and he added that it was likely that the performance next quarter also would be below expectations. He said that his nephew vowed to make immediate changes to personnel and that the firm would again be on track within six months. He said he was telling me all of this now so that I wouldn't worry.

Before Uncle Zhou finished getting the words out of his mouth, several thoughts occurred to me. At the time, I had been involved in almost daily meetings with the CEO and other executives at the firm to review any and all issues related to the operation and performance of the company, and I would report these facts back to Tom. So it was clear that this issue had been percolating for some time; the CEO received daily financial reports from accounting and knew about every issue facing the firm. This didn't just happen all of a sudden. It was also clear to me that the firm's accounting department was hardly to blame. It was a convenient foil for this conversation, as he wasn't about to point a finger at his nephew or at any other members of the family.

I found out later that Uncle Zhou's nephew—the CEO—didn't want to tell me that two quarters worth of financial data that was just given to me was incorrect. If he told me this himself, he would be embarrassed at such a stark demonstration of incompetence and surely would have lost face with me. To a Westerner, it seems ridiculous that the CEO would have his uncle deliver this news rather than doing so himself. To us, the result is virtually the same, and I would lack confidence in the CEO and his ability to manage his firm no matter who relayed the information to me. The Chinese don't view situations like this in the same way, however. Because Uncle Zhou conveyed the information, I should still have confidence in the CEO and in his ability to get the company back on track. Other people made the error, and he would correct it. As a result, the CEO didn't lose face, and I was informed about the disappointing performance—a very typical Chinese approach to this sort of situation.

Chinese culture is in many ways *form* over *substance*. The bravado of *ceremony*, the obligation of *saving face*, and the significance of *appearance* are business and cultural requisites. Every time I've been given a Chinese business plan to evaluate, I've been assaulted by proud, self-important descriptions and bold, grand images. To the Chinese, image and appearance are on par with substance and fact. And so on that day, signing the letter of intent was not so much about the letter itself, which possessed little significance from a legal standpoint. Rather, it was the ceremony surrounding the signing that was important. If Tom refused to sign the letter, then Mr. Wong would lose face with his family and (as we later found out) with the important Chinese government officials he brought along while we toured the AutoStar facilities.

Mr. Li quickly sensed from Tom's expression and hesitation that he was uncomfortable about signing the letter of intent. Without much more than a slight pause, Mr. Li quickly followed that it would be fine with Mr. Wong if the letter was nonbinding. The important thing for Mr. Wong, Ken explained to us later, was not the letter of intent itself but the ceremony surrounding the signing. As we soon would learn, the lavish event and celebratory banquet would occur in the presence of important Beijing political leaders and would be covered by Chinese print and TV media.

Tom, Ken, and I stepped into an adjoining room for a few moments to discuss the situation. Tom agreed that as long as he could write the letter himself (to ensure that it was nonbinding and had multiple disclaimers written into it), signing the letter at the ceremony should be okay. Upon hearing the news from Tom, Mr. Li's face beamed like a traditional Chinese red lantern, and he rushed off to inform Mr. Wong. Since the ceremony and banquet were to begin soon, Tom quickly penned the vaguest letter of intent I had personally ever read and presented it to Mr. Li for translation into Chinese.[14]

---

[14] When presenting any document, gift, business card, or other item, according to Chinese tradition, it is best to do so with both hands together holding the article, arms extended in front of the body. This way of presentation demonstrates thoughtfulness and respect, according to Chinese culture.

Later that afternoon we arrived at the signing ceremony to find that several copies of the letter of intent had been reproduced in both Chinese and English and were printed on distinctive ceremonial rice paper. Resting on top of each copy were meticulously placed Mont Blanc pens. Gorgeous flower arrangements rested upon the fine golden silk cover that was draped gracefully over the table. Behind the table sat two enormous black cherry wooden chairs with dragons ornately carved into the backrests and arms. To the left and right of the two center chairs, several elegant but less elaborate chairs were placed to accommodate seating for both parties. The right side was designated for Mr. Wong and his associates; the left side was designated for our team. Each seat had a name card folded into the shape of a teepee with our names written in Chinese on one side and in English on the other. Surrounding the signing table were nearly a dozen Chinese officials of apparent importance. Several photographers were snapping photo after photo as we arrived and took our assigned seats.

At the time, we were all astounded that the ceremony surrounding the endorsement of this simple, nonbinding letter of intent had assumed the atmosphere of the signing of an international treaty. The signing itself took no more than five minutes, with Mr. Wong and Tom each standing to say a few words of thanks and expressing optimism about the future. Immediately after each principal had signed the letter, several stunningly beautiful young women dressed in traditional Chinese red silk gowns presented all participants with flowers and gifts to mark the occasion. Our hosts also presented us with extra gifts to give to our colleagues at home that could not make the trip and attend the event. In fact, we received so many gifts that every one of us had to purchase an extra suitcase so that we could haul our mementos back home.

The evening celebration, attended by government officials and the entire Wong family, was a lavish gala that would have impressed any head of state. The following day we left Beijing.

CHAPTER 3 ═══════

Assembling the Deal

The first thing Tom did when we got back home was to convene a meeting with his partners at ABC Capital to discuss the AutoStar proposal. Back in 2005, the American real estate market was still hot, and the news coming out of China in the world and business press was all about opportunity. I didn't know it at the time, but even before I approached them, my friends at ABC Capital already had been thinking about investing in China and had started to look for opportunities there. After our trip, Tom was convinced more than ever that ABC Capital ought to commit a portion of its portfolio to China, and AutoStar potentially seemed to be an ideal initial target.

After several rounds of discussion based on the business and financial package Tom had brought back with him from China, the leadership at ABC Capital decided they should continue to press forward with AutoStar. In the United States, when ABC decided to finance a company, the decision was pretty straightforward. Once the initial contacts were made, the fund would ask for a GAAP audit and other due diligence data. Both sides would sit down and negotiate the terms. Assuming the results of those initial steps were successful, the fund would run the deal by its attorneys and CPAs. They would, of course, perform their own due diligence. If the lawyers and accountants signed off, they were in business. As for me, I've negotiated financing for companies all over the world—Europe, South America, and Latin America—and I've experienced the local cultures and business practices of companies from Norway to Brazil and from Switzerland to Japan. Based on my many years of experience, I thought the AutoStar deal would proceed in more or less the same way. Boy, was I wrong! All of my past experience didn't begin to prepare me for what was about to come.

Having made the decision to move forward, I met with Tom and the other guys at ABC Capital to discuss how we would proceed. ABC Capital was impressed with AutoStar and its management, and the automotive maintenance and repair business in China seemed to be an area that was experiencing substantial growth. In addition, they thought that this was a perfect time and opportunity to get into China. They had invested in businesses in most other areas of the world. The China market seemed like the next logical next step in their international growth model. They were anxious to proceed.

At our meeting, I was tasked by ABC Capital with amassing any information they requested so that they could follow through with the investment. I was then to coordinate whatever had to be accomplished with both AutoStar and ABC Capital. Because I knew nothing at all about doing business in China, I thought the first logical step would be to engage a knowledgeable attorney with expertise in Chinese law to advise me about how I should begin. For example, I didn't know what form of business entity should be used or formed or even how to go about setting it up. I also knew nothing about the Chinese legal system, such as how to conform contracts to Chinese law; nor did I know the first thing about the intricacies of Chinese accounting practices or financial statements.

Since I didn't personally know of a US law firm with offices in China, I called my friend Dave, who is an attorney at a large and respected international law firm we'll call Global Legal. I didn't know whether Dave's law firm had an office in China, but I knew that he could point me in the right direction if they didn't. As luck would have it, Dave told me that his law firm did indeed have an office in Beijing and that the managing partner of that office was born and educated in China and spent about half of her time in Beijing and the other half in Washington DC. Dave said he would set up a conference call to arrange an introduction. Dave told me that the attorney's name was Vera and that she had been born in China and received her undergraduate degree at a famous university in

Beijing.[15] After earning her undergraduate degree in China, Vera went to law school in the United States. She was in her mid-forties now, single, and her parents still lived in Beijing. I was in business!

A few days later Dave made the introduction. The following week, Vera called me from Beijing to talk specifically about the deal. After some initial chitchat about China and the weather in Florida, Vera asked me to provide her with a copy of any relevant documentation we had in our possession so that she could study it to get a better understanding of the planned transaction. She wanted to identify the goals and objectives on both sides and—in the end—she wanted to know precisely what we wanted to accomplish. After I hung up, I immediately copied everything I had and sent it to her for her review.

By now, about two weeks after we returned from our trip, I was having daily conversations with Tom at ABC Capital so that we were in sync with each other's activities. Through Ken, I was also having regular conversations with Mr. Wong. It was clear from the tone and content of our discussions that Mr. Wong was keenly interested in determining whether and when we would provide the required funding for his growing, cash-hungry company.

During the next several weeks, I explained in my many e-mails and phone conversations with Vera that the goals and objectives of the various parties were fairly straightforward. The desired outcome from this transaction for ABC Capital was to make money for the company, the fund, and its shareholders by taking the company public and eventually profiting on the sale of the stock. For AutoStar and Mr. Wong, the goal was to secure adequate funding as quickly as possible to support growth and expansion, and Mr. Wong was willing to give up a substantial equity position in the firm he created in order to accomplish that goal. Ken's

---

[15]   In China, many Chinese assume an English name when doing business with Westerners because of the difficulty most Westerners have in pronouncing Chinese names. For example, my longtime Chinese assistant and interpreter's first name in Chinese is Jingjie, but she goes by the name Maria to everyone but her immediate family.

objective was to be part of the transaction and to be given a small number of shares as a finder's fee. As for me, I would also receive restricted stock in the company for being an intermediary for ABC and coordinating between ABC, the company, and other professionals involved in the transaction. I was happy with that arrangement. I viewed it as a firsthand opportunity to learn more about working with and funding companies in China.

Based on our conversations, her review of the documents, and additional research, Vera advised us that the best way to structure our transaction was through an international joint venture (IJV). According to Vera, the two most common types of IJVs employed in China were equity joint ventures (EJVs) and cooperative joint ventures (CJVs). CJVs and EJVs are similar in many respects. For example, the government approval process, the basic format of the agreements, the tax status, and the legal framework for settling disputes were identical. Furthermore, the general management structure and governance procedures were essentially the same.

Vera explained that a Chinese equity joint venture (EJV) is a joint venture between a Chinese company and a foreign company within the territory of China. Both companies must invest in the joint venture, with the foreign company making not less than 25% of the total investment. EJVs are generally formed as limited liability companies (LLCs) in which the (equity) investor is not personally liable for the debts that the joint company might undertake in the future. In addition, an EJV has all of the rights and obligations of a legal Chinese person. As a result, an EJV is capable of buying land, hiring Chinese employees independently, constructing buildings, and so on.

However, Vera said that based on her experience, her review of the information we provided, and the objectives of both parties, she felt strongly that a cooperative (or contractual) joint venture (CJV) would better suit our needs, mainly because it allowed for greater negotiation of terms. A CJV could potentially reduce our risk exposure by helping ABC Capital to maintain greater control by negotiating the structure of management and staffing and by establishing voting rights into the articles of association. Because these rights do not have to be allocated according to equity stakes, as in an EJV, forming a CJV would provide

ABC Capital with greater flexibility. Also, because all of the terms are negotiated, CJVs can further help to reduce risk by forcing both sides to establish their respective rights and responsibilities in advance. Because the Chinese government must approve all CJVs formed in China, every CJV is essentially government sanctioned, which tends to deter Chinese partner noncompliance and provide greater legal recourse in case of noncompliance or fraud.[16]

Impressed by Vera's seemingly thorough understanding of the issues and her comprehensive explanation of our options, I thought we had found appropriate legal representation to help us put our deal together. I took the documents and summaries that Vera had given me to Tom and suggested that we arrange a conference call with her. The attorney and deal structure were critical elements of the transaction. I wanted Tom to speak to Vera directly and ask her anything that was on his mind. I wanted him to be sure. No doubts. This would be a key player in helping make his first transaction in China successful. As I sat with Tom during that conference call early the next morning, I knew by looking at Tom's face less than five minutes into the conversation that we had our attorney. He was every bit as impressed with Vera as I was. As a next step, we asked Vera to estimate how much she thought it would cost for Global Legal to represent us and to take us through the joint venture creation process from beginning to end.

Several days later, Vera called me back. She told me that after meeting with her partners and estimating the resources they would have to commit to this transaction, Global Legal would be willing to assemble the deal for about US $100,000. Vera said this price also would include a feasibility study analyzing the potential of this joint venture, along with due diligence on AutoStar and a background check on the principals, including Mr. Wong.

---

[16]   For a detailed discussion of the merits of cooperative joint ventures, see Paul H. Folta, "Cooperative Joint Ventures: Savvy foreign investors may wish to consider the benefits of this flexible investment structure," *The China Business Review Online,* http://www.chinabusinessreview.com/public/0501 /folta.html. This page was last accessed May 1, 2011.

Because I had no benchmark in China with which to assess the fairness of Global Legal's fee, I called Tom and relayed Vera's estimate to him. It turned out that Tom had no better idea than I did. He did say that it was significantly more than what he pays for similar services when working with American firms and even a bit more than what he pays when working on other international transactions. However, because he had no experience at all in making investments in Chinese firms, and since this firm was one of the best international law firms in the world, Tom decided to hire Global Legal and move forward.

Soon after that conversation, and just when I thought everything was on track, the first (of many) unexpected complications with this investment in the "Middle Kingdom" began to unfold.[17] Since the beginning of this journey, Tom assumed that he and ABC Capital would assume the role of equity investor. Since I was the person assigned to run point and was the main liaison with Global Legal, Vera was under the same impression. However, as soon as Vera began a conversation with ABC Capital's legal team, it quickly became apparent that, for a variety of reasons, ABC Capital would not or could not be a partner to the joint venture. This really threw me for a loop! I was expecting complications from Mr. Wong

---

[17]   For those of you that did not already know, the Chinese do not call their country China. Rather, the Chinese call their country Zhongguo, which in English can be literally translated as "Middle Kingdom." Zhong (中) means "middle" or "center" while guo (国) means "country" or "kingdom." This name is old, dating back three thousand years to the Chou Dynasty in 1,000 BC. The Chou people, unaware at the time of comparably advanced civilizations in the West, believed their empire occupied the middle of the earth, surrounded by barbarians. In many ways, this ethnocentric view the ancient Chinese had of themselves was well justified. They were responsible for many notable inventions, including paper, gunpowder, the abacus, the compass, the seismograph, kites, wheelbarrows, and many other things. The ancient Chinese also created indelible philosophies and religions such as Taoism, Buddhism, and Confucianism. Ancient Chinese art and artifacts today are esteemed and valued throughout the world. For more about China and its history, see its Wikipedia profile page at http://en.wikipedia.org /wiki/China. This page was last accessed May 1, 2011.

and the Chinese side, but this was the last thing I expected from our side. This brings me to Refkin's Rule #6: Expect the unexpected.

Refkin's Rule #6: Expect the unexpected. When doing business in China, always expect the unexpected. There are always exceptions to any rule.

Exasperated at the prospect of everything falling apart after having invested a considerable amount of my own time and money in this project already, I immediately asked for a phone conference between me, Tom, Vera, and Ken. During the conversation, Tom told us that ABC Capital could not fund AutoStar at the current time or be AutoStar's joint venture partner. We had to find another joint venture partner for AutoStar. Since I was the designated middleman for all of the activities between ABC Capital, AutoStar, and Global Legal, it was agreed that I should use my best efforts to try and identify a third-party American partner that was willing to form a joint venture with AutoStar.

The problem, of course, was that I didn't know of any such partner or even how to go about finding one! Where would you even start to look? Without a new joint venture partner we weren't going anywhere; that part was obvious.

As I usually do when I'm faced with an unfamiliar challenge, I immersed myself in the task at hand and began by doing some of my own research and by calling my friends and associates in business and investment banking to help me generate ideas and identify options. Unfortunately, it quickly became apparent that finding the right US-based corporate partner was going to be extremely difficult, at best. The companies I was able to identify as potential candidates were either too large or too small. The large national or multinational firms I spoke with had no interest at all in our relatively small and risky investment project. The smaller firms I spoke with were focused on domestic or European investments—on markets that were more established, had longer track records, and were better understood and less risky. All of the firms I spoke with understood the enormous opportunities available in China. However, the significant challenges of language, distance, and culture kept them closer to home.

Before long, the mounting series of rejections made me realize that if we were to take advantage of this opportunity, we'd have to form a company and assemble our own management team. With the advice and assistance of our attorneys, we created a company to represent the US side of the international joint venture. We'll call that company Plymouth Corporation.

In my effort to identify the right person with the right skills and background that could assume the role of managing partner of Plymouth and make the decisions for the joint venture, I knew exactly who I would ask first. I turned to my good friend Ned, who I knew had experience in the auto industry and who was familiar with the Chinese business environment. After speaking with Ned at some length about the project and its potential, Ned immediately said he liked the idea of being involved, mainly because he really understood it. AutoStar's focus was on automotive maintenance and repair, and Ned owned a business that manufactured and sold additives and car care products in the United States. It seemed like a good fit. Tom already knew Ned and also thought it was a good fit. So I called Ken and asked him to arrange a meeting with Mr. Wong at AutoStar so that I could introduce him to Ned. The next day, Ned and I booked our flights to Beijing.

Not even four weeks after returning from my first trip to China, I found myself once again soaring over the North Pole at six hundred miles an hour on a fourteen-hour United flight from Chicago to Beijing.[18] I couldn't believe it. Still, I was excited and couldn't wait to get back to China and work on this exciting and promising project. In honesty, it wasn't *only* the business opportunity that I was keyed up about. Although it had only been about a month, I couldn't wait to get back to China. I already missed the incredible food, outstanding hospitality, customer service, and the buzzing mass of humanity that overwhelmed my senses.

---

[18] Since that first trip to China in early 2005, I have flown to China on business almost every month, spending two weeks in China and three weeks in the United States. Before 2005, if anyone had told me that I would be spending almost 40% of my time in China during the next few years, I would have told them they were nuts.

When we arrived in Beijing the following morning, Ned and I had a lengthy meeting with the AutoStar team and toured its facilities. Just as it had with me, the scale and explosiveness of China and obvious potential of AutoStar blew Ned away. Although he had been doing business with Chinese firms in the United States and knew lots of other people who did business in China or with Chinese companies, Ned was speechless in his realization of just how capitalistic China was and how much potential it held as a consumer market. "Sure, I've heard all of the stories and read all of the articles," said Ned, "but no matter how much news you see or how many articles you read, you just can't imagine what's going on here until you actually see if for yourself." I smiled and nodded in agreement.

After meeting with AutoStar and discussing the opportunity with me later that evening, Ned eagerly agreed to manage the US side of the joint venture. He was fully on board before we departed for our trip back home. "The only precondition I would make," he said, "is that I also would be able to sell my auto care products in the Chinese market through AutoStar." Ned clearly understood China's potential as a consumer market in general and as a market for his auto care products in particular. He saw his involvement in this joint venture both as a way to earn income as a manager and as a way to distribute his products in the exploding Chinese auto market.

As soon as I returned from my trip, I had a meeting with ABC Capital's attorneys to review my plan. Unfortunately, when I told them that Ned agreed to act as the general manager as long as he could distribute his product line through the joint venture, the attorneys cut me off, telling me allowing Ned to do so would result in a serious conflict of interest that could result in legal complications down the road. Ned could manage Plymouth or sell his products to the joint venture, but not both, they told me.

I couldn't believe it. After investing the time and incurring the cost of another trip to China to recruit the perfect candidate to run Plymouth, I had to start all over again. I knew there was no talking Ned out of selling his products through AutoStar. He expressed to me clearly that distributing his products was his primary motivation for agreeing to manage the joint venture. So I still needed to find a person who was a strong organizer, who could effectively manage the partnership, and who would have no conflict of interest. That person, as it turned out, would be Scott.

Scott was a successful real estate developer and entrepreneur who had never been to China but who was smart, meticulously organized, and goal driven. He was exactly the kind of person who would take charge of the joint venture and keep it on track. As it turned out, Scott was the perfect choice. No detail ever escaped him, and he always gave 110% effort.

As soon as Scott agreed, I knew I had to take him to Beijing as soon as possible so that he could meet with Mr. Wong and better understand AutoStar and the Chinese auto services market. We immediately booked a flight from Florida to Beijing by way of Atlanta. Once we got to Atlanta, we shuttled to the international concourse, where we were to get new boarding passes for our connecting flight to Beijing on a foreign carrier.

The flight from Florida to Atlanta went off without a hitch. When we arrived at the check-in counter in Atlanta, I handed the ticket agent my passport. He verified the passport and visa and issued my boarding pass. When it was Scott's turn, the ticket agent flipped through his passport and then asked him if he could help find his visa. Without a thought or hesitation, Scott pulled out his wallet and handed the agent a Visa card, thinking that he had to pay some sort of fee. I immediately understood the problem. Having been to China twice already, I was aware that it was necessary to obtain a Chinese visa—a permission slip from the Chinese Embassy—to enter China. Somehow in my haste, I had forgotten all about helping Scott get his visa. I had given him the visa application to fill out but had forgotten to get it back from him so I could send it off for processing. I may have found the perfect managing partner for Plymouth/AutoStar, but he wasn't going with me to Beijing that day.

As I flew to Beijing, Scott headed back to Florida to wait for his visa. Although Scott applied for a rush order to obtain his visa, it took several days to get it. He then rebooked his flight and finally joined me in Beijing five days later.

The day after he landed, I took Scott with me on a tour of AutoStar's headquarters and to several of its service facilities. After speaking at length with Mr. Wong and touring AutoStar, Scott was as impressed as I thought he'd be. Scott told me he would be excited to assume the role of managing director of Plymouth, the US portion of the joint venture. "Step one accomplished!" I thought to myself. Finally!

Although securing the right manager for the partnership was a critical first step, successfully completing the next phase required to bring this project to fruition would prove to be even more critical and far more challenging to accomplish. While in China with Scott, I had been in constant contact with Tom at ABC Capital. As I had anticipated, based on my years of experience in raising capital for growing firms, Tom told me that (of course) before any funds would be forthcoming from the fund, it was essential that AutoStar supply GAAP-audited financial statements by a reputable and accredited international accounting firm. Tom added that, while he didn't need the GAAP audit immediately, sooner would be better than later.

After talking with Tom, Scott and I immediately asked for a meeting with Mr. Wong to discuss the accounting issue. To my great surprise, Mr. Wong said that he already had engaged an outside auditor to prepare audited statements. Even more astonishing, he said that he expected to have a complete set of audited financial statements available within a week. Impressed, I asked Mr. Wong to provide me with background and contact information on the accounting firm to pass along to Tom and ABC Capital. "Without this information," I told Mr. Wong, "ABC Capital could not possibly move forward with the transaction." Within hours, Mr. Wong provided me with the information I needed, translated into English, which I immediately faxed to Tom.

Almost a week to the day after my conversation with Mr. Wong, I received a package containing audited financial statements for the current year as well as for the past two years. The audit carried the Beijing accounting firm's official stamp, verifying the authenticity of the audit. Upon closer inspection of the actual figures, however, I noticed that the information in the statements was nearly identical to that given at the first presentation AutoStar made to us over two months ago. So either AutoStar's internal accounting staff was really good, or they simply arranged to have their auditor present the same information to us. At this point, I couldn't be sure, but I had to find out and pass that information along to Tom.

Looking back at that moment today, it seems obvious and clear that it would have been far better if we had invested more of our time researching and selecting the auditor ourselves to ensure that it was truly accurate and independent. At the time, however, we knew of no accounting firms in Beijing other than the Big Four.[19] The one audit firm I did know with a presence in Asia had their offices in Hong Kong, a backup that I would use if Mr. Wong's audit firm proved unacceptable.

Tom and I questioned Mr. Wong and his accounting staff about the values in the report and about the auditing firm selected to produce the statements. In the end, however, we relied on the audit report provided to us by AutoStar's accounting firm. Part of the reason we were willing to do so is that Mr. Wong's auditor provided us with its client reference list, which we had our attorneys check and verify (after calling those clients) as being accurate. In addition, our attorneys also went to the auditor's offices to verify the existence and location of the firm and found everything reported to us to be in order. As a result, at that point we had no reason not to believe in the validity of Mr. Wong's auditor's report.

A week later, I met with Vera from Global Legal, and she provided Tom and me with a thorough background analysis of Mr. Wong. Vera sent us the feasibility study report we had hired Global Legal to perform on AutoStar in general and on the desirability of forming the cooperative joint venture specifically. A summary feasibility study report is depicted in figure 4.

---

[19]   The Big Four are the four largest international accountancy and professional services firms, which handle the vast majority of audits for publicly traded companies as well as many private companies. The Big Four firms include Deloitte & Touche, PricewaterhouseCoopers, Ernst & Young, and KPMG. For more discussion of the Big Four, see the Wikipedia profile page at http://en.wikipedia.org/wiki/Big_Four_(audit_firms). This page was last accessed May 1, 2011.

In general, the feasibility study suggested that the automotive maintenance and repair market was a promising area for business growth within China. More importantly, it said that AutoStar was well positioned to take advantage of that growth and that expanding this business through the creation of a cooperative joint venture was promising. In addition, Mr. Wong's background checked out as advertised and gave no indication of any complaints against him, past or present. "Everything looks really solid," said Vera.

Figure 4

AutoStar Feasibility Study Report

July 5, 2005

AutoStar, Ltd. of the People's Republic of China ("Party A"), **ABC Capital** of the United States of America ("Party B") and Plymouth Group, LLC ("Party C") of the United States of America in accordance with the law of the People's Republic of China (PRC) on Chinese-Foreign Cooperative Joint Ventures and the related Regulations for the Implementation of the Law of the PRC on Chinese-Foreign Cooperative Joint Ventures (the "Joint Venture Law") and other relevant laws and regulations of the PRC, through friendly discussions and in conformity with the principles of equality and benefit for all parties have agreed to invest in and establish jointly a cooperative joint venture, **AutoStar Cooperative Joint Venture** (CJV), and formulate this Feasibility Study Report.

The purpose of this report is to specify the general business goals, scopes, and the principles of the CJV and to provide a framework for the business plan of the CJV thereof in order to procure investment in and provide all of the other elements of planned business activities and economic return of the CJV.

A. COOPERATIVE JOINT VENTURE PROJECT:

Name: **AutoStar Cooperative Joint Venture**
Country of Registration: PRC;
Legal Representative: ____**Mr. Wong**_____ ;
Nationality: PRC
Legal Address: ___**100 China Street, Beijing, P.R. China**.

B. INVESTORS OF PROPOSED PROJECT

(1) Party A
Name: ___**Mr. Wong**_____;
Country of Registration: The People's Republic of China ("PRC");
Legal representative: ___**Beijing Law Firm**_____;
Nationality: PRC
Legal Address: _____**200 China Street, Beijing, P.R. China**.
Party A is a company specializing in the comprehensive auto services industry in Beijing. The company is one of the top companies in the auto service industry in the country, and its business covers auto repair, auto maintenance, auto accessories supply, auto insurance related services, and other auto service related services. It has rich client resources and a solid rapidly growing business. It will bring its expertise, clients, and its business into the JV.

(2) Party B
Name: ___**ABC Capital**_____;
Country of Registration: Individual American citizen;
Nationality: U.S.A.
Legal Address: _____**100 America Road, America, Florida**.
Party B is an individual consultant who will provide consulting services regarding China markets, and geographic and social areas for the opportunities of opening new auto services centers of the JV throughout the country;

(3) <u>Party C</u>
Name: Plymouth Group, LLC;
Country of Registration: State of Delaware of the United States of America;
Legal Representative: ___ **Global Legal** ___;
Nationality: U.S.A.
Legal Address: ___ **200 America Road, New York, NY,** U.S.A.
Party C is a company specializing in ___ **legal services** ___.

C. <u>INTENTION OF THE PROPOSED PROJECT</u>

Along with the economic development in China, more and more automobiles have been involved in everyday life of the Chinese people. As a result, automobile maintenance related services have become greatly in need. Therefore, how to obtain the best technology and how to provide the fastest growth for automobile services have become a crucial subject of the auto market, especially at this moment when the country is preparing for the 2008 Beijing Olympic Games. Under such circumstances, Party A, Party B, and Party C of the CJV have agreed to work together to develop a new chain of automobile services centers ("the Project") in China to meet such need by using the most advanced technologies and best customer-oriented approaches. The CJV plans to establish sixty (60) auto services centers in Beijing for the first stage and then expand its operation to the other cities of the country.

D. <u>DETAILS OF PROPOSED PROJECT</u>

(1) <u>Business Scope</u>: Auto technological services, auto maintenance, auto body repair, auto accessories supply, and other auto related services.

(2) <u>Term</u>: The CJV has a twenty (20) years term which can be renewed upon the written agreement of the JV parties.

(3) <u>Number of Centers</u>: The CJV plans to open 60 auto services centers at the first stage of the operation in Beijing.

(4) <u>Number of Employees</u>: The CJV plans to employ about 900 employees for the centers; more employees may be added to meet the development of the operation.

(5) <u>Legal Address</u>:   300 China Street, Beijing, P.R. China   .

E. **TOTAL INVESTMENT, METHOD FOR REGISTERED CAPITAL**

1. Total Investment: **$8** million;

2. Registered Capital: **$24** million;

3. Method for Registered Capital contribution: The CJV will remit the registered capital by installments and the first amount of the registered of **$1.2** million will be contributed by the parties within three months after the business license will be issued. The rest of the installments will be contributed in a time frame and manner that the parties agree upon; and that are consistent with the existing Chinese foreign investment and cooperative joint venture laws and regulations.

F. **COMPANY STRUCTURE**

The CJV chooses to establish the board of directors which is the highest authority of the CJV. The board of directors shall decide all major issues concerning the CJV. The board of directors shall consist of seven directors, of which four shall be appointed by Party A, and three will be appointed by Party C. The Chairman of the board will be **Mr. Wong**. The CJV shall have a General Manager. The General Manager shall be appointed by the board of directors. The General Manager is directly responsible to the board of directors. He shall carry out the decisions of the board of directors, organize and conduct the daily production, technology and operation and management of the CJV.

G. <u>ENVIRONMENTAL AND LABOR SECURITY CONSIDERATIONS</u>

CJV operations will adopt necessary measures to follow the relevant rules regarding environmental and labor security protections, including "PRC Environmental Law," "PRC Labor Security Law" and other related laws and regulations.

H. <u>INVESTMENT & BENEFITS FORECAST</u>

1. <u>Equity Ownership Percentage</u>:

- Party A has **67.75** % equity ownership;
- Party B has **5.0** % equity ownership; and
- Party C has **27.25** % equity ownership.

2. <u>Capital Contribution</u>

- The estimated total investment of the JV is **$29.45** million;

- The estimated registered capital commitment is **$11.78** million;

- Party A plans to contribute $ **20** million by providing equipment, facilities and houses, car insurance clients and related data bases, and new technology, know-how and other types of intellectual properties without cash contribution;

- Party C plans to contribute **$8** million by providing cash;

- Party B plans to contribute $**1.45** million by providing consulting services for the JV without any capital contribution;

- All of the parties understand that the amount of the total investment and the registered capital for the JV may be increased in the future, due to the necessities of the development and the expansion of the CJV.

3. Investment Assessment

Building 40 small auto centers: US$4 million ($100,000 x 40)
Building 10 medium centers: US$2.5 million ($250,000 x 10)
Building 10 large centers: US$4 million ($400,000 x 10)

4. Benefit forecast

Daily revenue for each small center is no less than $1,200
Daily revenue for each medium center is no less than $3,000
Daily revenue for each large center is no less than $4,200
(Based on 250 working days a year)
The 1st to 2nd year's estimated revenue for small centers is $12 million;
The 1st to 2nd year's estimated revenue for medium centers is $7.5 million;
The 1st to 2nd year's estimated revenue for large centers is $10.5 million;
The 1st to 2nd year's estimated profit is
The 1st to 2nd year's distributable profit is

I. CONCLUSION

Based on the above analysis of the CJV's proposal to incorporate Sino-US Yunnan Auto Technological Services Limited, the proposed project indicates high market demand, strong clientele base, potential for fast growth, and attractive return on investment in the future. In conclusion, the feasibility of the proposed project, from an economic and social point of view indicates a favorable investment for the auto services industry in China.

Authorized Person

By:

Date:

After the meeting with Vera, I forwarded the documents to ABC Capital and reviewed them in detail with Tom and his team during a conference call. Because the audit, feasibility study, background check, and business plan seemed to be in good order and its prospects seemed promising, ABC Capital chose to cautiously move forward with the investment.

After getting the confirmation from Tom, I immediately called Vera and asked her to proceed with the preparation of the final documents and to tell her that I would introduce her to Mr. Wong, since it would be necessary for Global Legal to continue collecting information and vetting risks. I called Mr. Wong and explained that his cooperation with Global Legal was absolutely essential to the success of this project. In response, he declared that he and his family "would not sleep" until any requested information was in our hands.

Things were on track so far. However, there was one very important strategic and organizational issue to settle—how to take the merged company public on US financial markets. This was a key and essential issue for ABC Capital because the only way they could get their invested funds and profits back out of China in general and AutoStar specifically was through the sale of the merged firm's stock sometime after it went public. The real question was how to most efficiently and cost effectively take the CJV public in the US marketplace.

After considerable research, and consultation with Global Legal, it was decided to take the merged company public using a technique known as a *reverse merger* or *reverse takeover* (RTO). An RTO is a relatively simple, efficient, and cost-effective method by which a private company can become a public company.

Here's how it works. An RTO requires two companies: an operationally dormant publicly listed company with limited business opportunities or assets (commonly referred to as a "shell" company), and a private company with viable business opportunities and significant assets. The RTO occurs when the private company "reverse merges" into the already public company, which now becomes an entirely new operating entity and generally changes its name to reflect the newly merged company's business. The private company shareholders receive a majority of the shares of the public company and assume control of its board of directors. The transaction can be accomplished within weeks as long as both companies have current GAAP audited financial statements, and the shell company is current with its SEC filings. Since the shell is generally an SEC-registered company, the private company does not go through an expensive and time-consuming review with state and federal regulators because this process was completed beforehand with the public company. Figure 5 provides a flow chart detailing the path to a public US listing using a reverse takeover (RTO).

One of the most important advantages in using an RTO to take a company public, compared to a traditional IPO,[20] is that the initial costs (filing fees and attorney and investment banking fees) are much lower, and the time frame for taking the merged company public is considerably shorter. Advantages and disadvantages associated with going public through a reverse takeover are provided in figure 5.

---

[20]   The acronym IPO stands for initial public offering. An IPO is when a firm issues shares of common stock to the public for the first time. For further discussion of IPOs, see the Wikipedia profile page at http://en.wikipedia .org/wiki/Initial_public_offering. This page was last accessed May 1, 2011.

Figure 5

Advantages of Going Public through a Reverse Merger

Benefits of Going Public through the RTO (Reverse Takeover)

- Initial costs are much lower and excessive investment banking fees are avoided.
- The time frame for becoming public is considerably shorter.
- There is no significant regulatory review or regulatory approval for the transaction.
- The company can now use its stock as currency to finance acquisitions and attract quality management.
- Capital is easier to raise, as investors now have a clearly defined exit strategy through the public markets.

Some High-Profile and Successful RTOs

- **Armand Hammer,** world renowned oil magnate and industrialist, is generally credited with having invented the RTO. In the mid-1950s, Hammer invested in a shell company into which he merged multi-decade winner **Occidental Petroleum.**
- In 1970 **Ted Turner** completed a reverse merger with failing Rice Broadcasting, which went on to become **Turner Broadcasting.**
- In 1996, **Muriel Siebert**, renowned as the first woman member of the New York Stock Exchange, took her brokerage firm public by reverse merging with J. Michaels, a defunct Brooklyn furniture company.
- One of the dot-com fallen angels, **Rare Medium (NASDAQ: RRRR)**, merged with a marginal refrigeration company. This was a $2 stock in 1998, which found its way over $90 in 2000.

- **Aklaim Entertainment (NASDAQ: AKLM)** merged into non-operating Tele-Communications Inc. in 1994.

Negatives of Going Public through the RTO

- There may be no capital raised in conjunction with going public.
- There is limited sponsorship for the stock, and the stock generally trades on a lower level, i.e., the Pink Sheets or Bulletin Board.
- There is no high-powered Wall Street investment banking relationship.

We did run into one additional complication. In a typical US-based reverse merger, both the private company and the shell company are combined to form one public company. Vera explained that according to Chinese law, it was not possible to simply dissolve the cooperative joint venture into the new company in China. We could not simply merge the joint venture with the shell and have it disappear. Fortunately, after a bit of thought and research, Global Legal devised a workable solution that would satisfy the legal and regulatory authorities in both the United States and China. We would merge 95% of the joint venture's assets into the shell company to create the new, publicly listed firm. The remaining 5% of the Plymouth/AutoStar joint venture would remain outside the publicly listed firm as a Chinese/US cooperative joint venture.

After resolving the legal and financial issues required to take the joint venture public using an RTO, our next task was to identify and negotiate terms with a viable publicly listed shell company.[21] As luck would have it,

---

[21] A viable shell company is one that publicly traded and is current in its Securities and Exchange Commission (SEC) filings. Shell companies typically are microcap stocks (publicly traded companies that have a market capitalization of roughly US $250 million or less). Most microcap firms are traded over the counter (OTC), and their prices are quoted on the OTC Bulletin Board (OTCBB) or the Pink Sheets.

Tom knew of a viable American publicly listed microcap shell company that was currently looking for suitors. Tom told me that as far as he knew, the company was current in all SEC filings and had twenty-six thousand shareholders (although, as we later found out, many of these shareholders held very few shares), a staggering number for a microcap OTCBB company. Figure 6 contains a partial reproduction of the Securities and Exchange Commission guide to microcap stocks.[22]

Figure 6
U.S. Securities and Exchange Commission:
Microcap stock: A guide for investors

What Is a Microcap Stock?

The term "microcap stock" applies to companies with low or "micro" capitalizations, meaning the total value of the company's stock. Microcap companies typically have limited assets. For example, in cases where the SEC suspended trading in microcap stocks, the average company had only $6 million in net tangible assets—and nearly half had less than $1.25 million. Microcap stocks tend to be low priced and trade in low volumes.

Where Do Microcap Stocks Trade?

Many microcap stocks trade in the "over-the-counter" (OTC) market and are quoted on OTC systems, such as the OTC Bulletin Board (OTCBB) or the "Pink Sheets."

[22] Securities Exchange Guide to Microcap Stocks. http://www.sec.gov/investor/pubs/microcapstock.htm. This website was accessed on May 27, 2008.

- **OTC Bulletin Board**—The OTCBB is an electronic quotation system that displays real-time quotes, last-sale prices, and volume information for many OTC securities that are not listed on the Nasdaq Stock Market or a national securities exchange. Brokers who subscribe to the system can use the OTCBB to look up prices or enter quotes for OTC securities. Although the NASD oversees the OTCBB, the OTCBB is *not* part of the Nasdaq Stock Market. Fraudsters often claim that an OTCBB company is a NASDAQ company to mislead investors into thinking that the company is bigger than it is.

- **The "Pink Sheets"**—The Pink Sheets, named for the color of paper on which they've historically been printed, are listings of price quotes for companies that trade in the over-the-counter market (OTC market). "Market makers" are the brokers that commit to buying and selling the securities of OTC issuers, and they can use the pink sheets to publish bid and ask prices. A company named Pink Sheets LLC, formerly known as the National Quotation Bureau, publishes the Pink Sheets in both hard copy and electronic format. Pink Sheets LLC is not registered with the SEC as a stock exchange, and the SEC does not regulate its activities.

How Are Microcap Stocks Different from Other Stocks?

- **Lack of Public Information**—The biggest difference between a microcap stock and other stocks is the amount of reliable, publicly available information about the company. Larger public companies file reports with the SEC that any investor can get for free from the SEC's website. Professional stock analysts regularly research and write about larger public companies, and it's easy to find their stock prices in the newspaper. In contrast, information about microcap companies can be extremely difficult to find, making them more vulnerable to investment fraud schemes.

- **No Minimum Listing Standards**—Companies that trade their stocks on major exchanges and in the Nasdaq Stock Market must meet minimum listing standards. For example, they must have minimum amounts of net assets and minimum numbers of shareholders. In contrast, companies on the OTCBB or the Pink Sheets do not have to meet any minimum standards.

- **Risk**—While all investments involve risk, microcap stocks are among the most risky. Many microcap companies tend to be new and have no proven track record. Some of these companies have no assets or operations. Others have products and services that are still in development or have yet to be tested in the market. Another risk that pertains to microcap stocks involves the low volumes of trades. Because microcap stocks trade in low volumes, any size of trade can have a large percentage impact on the price of the stock.

A few days later, Tom arranged for me to call Michael and Matthew—two likable guys we wound up referring to as the M&M brothers—the managers and majority owners of the shell company that we'll call Deep Doo Doo Inc. When I called, I happened to get Matthew on the phone. Matthew told me that he and Tom had already discussed the possibility of combining their company with a Chinese company and that he would be interested in allowing us to merge the joint venture with Deep Doo Doo if the terms were right. He told me that the first thing he needed was a copy of the joint venture's financial statements so that he could better understand the opportunities and risks involved. That afternoon I sent Matt a complete package. It seemed like everything was coming together.

That night I arranged a conference call between me, Mr. Wong, Vera (who acted in the additional role of translator), and Tom. Because the merger would require a significant investment in time and money, we wanted to make sure that Mr. Wong completely understood what was involved in merging with Deep Doo Doo in order to take the AutoStar/

Plymouth joint venture public. We also wanted to be absolutely certain that Mr. Wong had ample opportunity to ask any questions that he might have about the investment and the process. During the conversation, Vera went over the agreement, carefully laying out the terms, the risks and rewards, and the expectations and responsibilities of all parties. Tom also explained the process of using a reverse merger to take the company public and told Vera and Mr. Wong that we already were in the process of evaluating a public shell company candidate.[23]

Rarely interrupting to ask questions, Mr. Wong listened quietly and patiently. I thought it was rather strange that Mr. Wong asked almost no questions during the call despite the relative complexity of the issues being discussed and the importance and impact they would have for him and for AutoStar. I suddenly began to get a bit nervous. I'd been involved in many conference calls like this during my long career, and, based on my experience, a lack of questioning from one of the principals is never a good sign. Usually, it reflects either embarrassment at not understanding the issues being discussed or, worse, not caring about the issues being discussed.

---

[23] This was prior to September 2006, when China's State Administration of Foreign Exchange issued a rule entitled Circular 106, which went into effect in the summer of 2007. This new rule requires Chinese companies that set up offshore entities for domestic investment to receive approval from Chinese regulators prior to establishing such offshore jurisdiction. At first it was anticipated that the new rule was established to halt China-based companies from going public outside of China, but this was not the case. In 2007, sixty-nine companies went public in the United States using a reverse merger. This number represents almost 33% of the total number of reverse mergers in 2007 and reflects a 30% year-to-year increase, with twenty-eight mergers in the fourth quarter of 2007 alone. The Chinese deals as an aggregate were valued at almost $1.5 billion, with a third of those numbers occurring in the fourth quarter of 2007. The Chinese reverse mergers are very appealing to funding sources because the valuations of the companies are funded at low PE ratios and thus provide substantial upside for potential investors. I believe we will see a substantial number of new deals coming out of China in 2008. Additionally, deals from other parts of Asia are starting to trickle into the US markets. For further discussion on this topic, see the website Reverse Shell Mergers Explained: Everything you wanted to know about Reverse Shell Mergers, by Ralph Amato. http://reverseshellmerger.com/category /china/. This page was last accessed on July 18, 2008.

In most of my successful deals, there were plenty of questions on both sides and the parties worked together to resolve issues and move forward as a team. The complete lack of inquiry on behalf of Mr. Wong left me feeling very uneasy. Finally, as we were wrapping up the conversation, Vera asked all of us if we had any last questions before we hung up. To my surprise, Mr. Wong suddenly spoke in a clear and deliberate voice to Vera. Although I didn't fully understand the conversation until it was interpreted a few minutes later, I immediately sensed what Mr. Wong was asking. He wanted to know when he would get the money. (Remember Refkin's Rule #3.) After Vera interpreted his question to us, Tom responded by emphasizing that ABC Capital still was a very long way from completing its corporate and financial due diligence and that we still had substantial work to do to structure the reverse merger. Once translated, Tom's response elicited no reaction by Mr. Wong, ending our conversation. A few weeks later, Tom, Ken, Scott, and I flew back to Beijing. With great ceremony and celebration, we met with Vera and Mr. Wong and his team and signed the joint venture agreement. All of the joint venture documents were translated in triplicate into both English and Chinese by Global Legal. Before the signatures were dry, the documents were whisked off to be registered with the relevant Chinese government authority, making the deal "official." So what did these signatures mean? Well, by signing the cooperative joint venture agreement, Plymouth was legally obligated to infuse AutoStar with $8 million in registered capital in exchange for a 27.25% ownership of the joint venture. Mr. Wong and his company would contribute nearly $20 million in assets and have a 67.5% ownership position in the joint venture. The remaining 5% interest would belong to Ken in exchange for his assistance in putting the parties together. Although Plymouth was obligated to deliver the funds, the timing of the infusion was not specified; so it was at Plymouth's option. From Plymouth's perspective, there was no need to rush. ABC Capital would be funding Plymouth on the US side of the joint venture. Plymouth, in turn, would be transferring the $8 million in operating capital to AutoStar to open more stores and expand the business. This meant that Tom and the other principals at ABC Capital were obligated to their shareholders to take extraordinary care in determining the best use of proceeds, to adequately vet risks and alternatives, and to formulate an implementation process. At this point, we had pulled together all of the pieces necessary to make this deal work. The general relationship among the participants is illustrated in figure 7.

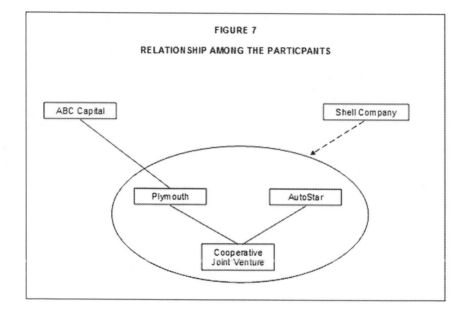

CHAPTER 4 ═══════

In China, It's Always All about the Money

Now that the formal documents had been signed and recorded, I was fully aware that the most important objective for Mr. Wong, from his perspective, was to get as much of the $8 million in capital as soon as possible. He knew that, to achieve this objective, he had to develop a strategy to justify an immediate and pressing need for the funds. The following paragraphs describe how his strategy played out.

The strategy Mr. Wong chose was initiated by a phone call to me by one of his staff requesting a visit to ABC Capital's offices in New York, arguing that it was important that he and his firm perform their own due diligence on ABC Capital. I was a bit surprised but nevertheless happy to forward his request to Tom. A bit amused, Tom told me to tell Mr. Wong that he and ABC Capital were more than happy to accommodate him and were in fact eager to reciprocate the hospitality shown to us during our visits to Beijing.

The day of Mr. Wong and his staff's New York visit arrived several weeks later. Amazingly, Mr. Wong and his entourage arrived with the same bluster and excitement that we had experienced on our trips to Beijing, hauling suitcases loaded with enough gifts for every member of the management and staff at ABC Capital. For its part, ABC Capital was equally prepared, presenting typical "American" gifts—a New York Yankees jacket for Mr. Wong, and caps, coffee cups, and other logo memorabilia stuffed into individual bags for each member of his entourage.

The day after they arrived, we immediately got down to business. In truth, our agenda didn't include anything of significant business importance. The trip and meetings we arranged for Mr. Wong and his entourage was more like a "state visit" rather than a business mission. Just before our meeting began, however, I was a bit surprised when Mr. Wong's cherubic nephew, Mr. Li, informed me that Mr. Wong had recently been presented with an extraordinary business opportunity and would like to add it to the meeting agenda as a point of discussion. Knowing that Tom would have no objections, I told Mr. Li that I thought Tom would be pleased to append it to the agenda. I went further, adding that the dialogue between Mr. Wong and the fund was open and that Mr. Wong should feel free to discuss anything he wished. Mr. Li was obviously elated, beaming in his usual jolly way.

During the meeting, the mood on the part of Mr. Wong and his team suddenly stiffened when he began to describe the new, incredible business opportunity he had recently been presented with. Mr. Wong began by telling ABC Capital that because of his political connections, the government was going to give him the opportunity to buy sixty government-owned automotive repair centers located throughout China for only $1.2 million. He continued, telling us that this was a very special agreement that resulted from his influence and past association with the government.[24] Then Mr. Wong's eyes narrowed and his tone and expression became more earnest. "But there is a problem," Mr. Wong continued, "and it is a problem I am reluctant to bring up, particularly during this time of joyous celebration." Then he continued. "In order to take advantage of this rare and fleeting opportunity," he said, "we are required to complete the transaction within the next two weeks."

---

[24]   In China, the importance of personal friendships and contacts in doing business—called guānxi (关系)—cannot be overstated. Guānxi describes a personal connection between two individuals in which one is able to prevail upon another to perform a favor or service. The two individuals need not be of equal social status. Guānxi is also used to describe a network of contacts that an individual can call upon when something needs to be done, and through which he or she can exert influence on behalf of another. For further discussion of Guanxi, see its Wikipedia profile at http://en.wikipedia.org /wiki/Guanxi. This page was last accessed on May 1, 2011.

Mr. Wong added that not only was the opportunity rare and fleeting, but also that his contacts in the government had gone out on a limb by giving him preferential treatment over a number of his competitors. "Our competition in the auto service and repair business would love to see us fail in our efforts so *they* can buy these centers from the government and drive us out of business!" exclaimed Mr. Wong. He then said that with this acquisition, "AutoStar would become the largest automotive repair operation in Beijing and soon in all of China! Unfortunately," Mr. Wong added, "We currently don't have the cash flow necessary to take advantage of this opportunity, so we need to ask you to advance $1.2 million of the total $8 million in capital now, rather than later."

Feeling unprepared to respond to this information, Tom said that he would need some time to collect and analyze the data concerning this transaction. Astonishingly, Mr. Li immediately produced the plans, including names of the facilities, financial projections, and other detailed information, and handed them to Tom. After briefly scanning the documents, Tom responded that he thought this opportunity looked very interesting but that he would have to consult with his team and get back to Mr. Wong. As the meeting ended, Mr. Wong again emphasized that the opportunity would be gone in two weeks, so he asked Tom to act quickly. This brings me to Refkin's Rule #7.

> **Refkin's Rule #7: Expect short time frames in which to think and act where money is concerned.** Whenever foreign businessmen are to provide capital to Chinese businessmen, the Chinese always minimize the period between when the request is made and delivery is due. Chinese businessmen never give the foreign partner long to think about the delivery of funds.

Looking back with the benefit of hindsight, it is clear that Mr. Wong's strategy was to get Tom to make a significant financial commitment to ensure that he couldn't easily back out of the deal in the event that he happened upon any unfavorable information. He knew very well that once Tom put serious money into the investment, the odds were far greater that Tom would remain committed through consummation of the deal.

The shorter the time given to make the investment, the greater the chance that Tom would feel compelled to provide the funding they sought if the cost of not doing so could result in a significant loss or a significant cost. In a typical business decision-making process, those responsible for making the decision generally prefer to think about the issue clearly, over a period of time, to reduce the possibility of error. Chinese businessmen typically try to limit the time between when the need to act is conveyed and when the action is required. The pressure requiring quick action, combined with severe consequences of inaction, tends to focus action in a single direction rather than to allow looking at a decision process more completely and objectively. Chinese businessmen know this, of course, and employ this strategy frequently and with great skill.

After returning home, Mr. Wong and various members of his family called ABC Capital almost daily, repeating their fear of losing the opportunity to purchase the government facilities that we had discussed. "The time to act is now!" they repeatedly stressed. In the meantime, ABC Capital forwarded copies of the documentation it had received about the government contracts to Global Legal for their comment and advice. After several days, Global Legal advised Tom that the contracts and projections that Mr. Wong had provided seemed to be sound, official, and in order. Relying on the due diligence performed by Global Legal, Tom instructed ABC Capital's in-house attorneys to draw up the necessary documents and contracts. After the documents were translated and signed, the $1.8 million was immediately deposited into Plymouth, and $1.2 million was wired from Plymouth to AutoStar. The additional $600,000 was left on deposit in Plymouth's account to cover the future audit, legal, and other expenses associated with a future public offering. Tom was confident that his money was well invested and that his ability to obtain the government-owned service centers at below-market rates would only enhance ABC Capital's return.

Everything seemed to be going smoothly until a few weeks after Mr. Wong's visit. I received a message through Maria from my now good friend Mr. Li telling me that it was urgent that he talk to me. I set up a call for the following day. The next day, soon after we began our discussion, and to my utter shock and dismay, Mr. Li told me that he was very sorry to tell us that Mr. Wong was unable to immediately purchase the government-owned service centers that ABC Capital wired the money for. He told me that Mr. Wong would still be able to buy these centers at some time in the future through the special deal he'd worked out with his friends at China's Ministry of Commerce. "We just can't do it now," he said. I immediately reacted with alarm. Sensing my distress, Mr. Li quickly and happily added, "But don't worry about the $1.2 million; Mr. Wong said he will use that money to fund the planned expansion of the current maintenance and repair facilities!" This brings me to Refkin's Rule # 8.

> **Refkin's Rule #8**: **Expect to get the "bad news" from a "friend."**
> Chinese businessmen will relay "bad news" to foreign business partners only as a last resort, and usually by utilizing a friend or someone the foreign partner likes or feels comfortable with. Once the foreign business partner does get the bad news, it is always relayed at the last possible moment to allow for the least amount of time for the foreign partner to think and to act.

After hanging up, I immediately called Tom and told him what Mr. Li had told me. Infuriated, Tom told me that he would convene a meeting to discuss this issue with his partners and that I was to get back to him the next day. Tom was extremely and justifiably upset. Here he had just wired $1.2 million to a bank account in China, and he didn't have a thing to show for it other than the contracts Global Legal had drawn up. After consulting with his in-house attorneys, Tom called me and told me to tell Mr. Wong to immediately return the money. Obviously prepared for Tom's demand for return of the money, Mr. Wong patiently explained that, according to the documents we had signed, the money was considered as registered capital and, unfortunately, could not be wired back.

When I told Tom how Mr. Wong had responded, he immediately called Vera at Global Legal to find out what his options were. "If we can't get the money back," Tom told Vera, "then I want your firm to verify that the money is being used to expand the company's facilities as Mr. Wong said."

As the attorneys studied the issue and our legal costs began to mount, we found out a short time later that Mr. Wong did indeed invest at least some part of the wired funds to expand AutoStar. Global Legal verified that Mr. Wong had leased space for additional service centers and that he bought equipment for those centers and hired workers to operate them. A few weeks later, at the insistence of ABC Capital, I returned to Beijing to verify the existence of the facilities firsthand. During my tour, I found that several of the new stores already were operational while others were still under *decoration*.[25]

After my visits to the new locations, I called Tom and reported that it appeared that what Mr. Wong had said, and Global Legal had confirmed, was true. AutoStar appeared to be using the funds to expand operations. As one would expect, Tom let out a huge sigh of relief at hearing this news and tensions began to ease somewhat afterward. However, both Tom and I agreed that there had better not be any more surprises like that again.

Sometime later, as the new AutoStar service centers were nearing completion, Mr. Wong called me to announce that he was planning a grand, formal signing ceremony to commemorate our cooperation and that this important event would be covered by all major Beijing news media—and that it would be held at the Great Hall of the People, no less![26] He said that he would be sending out formal invitations to everyone on our side of the deal but wanted to give me the good news early so that we could begin making plans to come. Still feeling betrayed and more than a little skeptical, I reluctantly told him that I would plan to attend.

The event was to take place a few weeks later on the afternoon of Thursday, November 10, 2005. "That is a very lucky day!" Mr. Wong exclaimed without elaborating. Preparations were made, and invitations were sent to anyone and everyone involved in the transaction, no matter how distant the connection.

---

[25] *Decoration* is the Chinese word used to describe tenant improvements.

[26] The *Great Hall of the People* or *Rénmín Dàhuìtáng* (人民大会堂) is located at the western edge of Tiananmen Square, Beijing, People's Republic of China, and is used for legislative and ceremonial activities by the People's Republic of China and the Communist Party of China. It functions as China's parliament building. For further information, see its Wikipedia profile page at http://en.wikipedia.org/wiki/Great_Hall_of_the_People. This page was last accessed on May 1, 2011.

The day prior to the event, I arrived in Beijing with Scott, and we were personally greeted by a beaming Mr. Wong at the airport. He obviously was excited and seemed genuinely happy to see us. The next day, on the morning of the event, a large crowd gathered as a caravan of luxury sedans lined up outside our hotel. With a motorcycle police escort and sirens blaring, we paraded slowly toward the Great Hall of the People. If Mr. Wong's objective was to impress, he accomplished the task with flying colors on that clear, cool November day. As we arrived at the Great Hall, we were greeted on its steps (I was told) by the vice chairman of the Standing Committee of the National People's Congress, Bu He.[27] During the ceremony, I was seated next to Mr. Bu, and we were both asked to give a short speech, which was simultaneously translated and broadcast live on CCTV.[28]

After the conclusion of the formal event at the Great Hall, which included a banquet fit for any head of state, we were escorted back to our cars and chauffeured to a large, new AutoStar service center that had recently completed renovations. During this part of the celebration, Mr. Wong had orchestrated a magnificent, formal ribbon-cutting ceremony that included music, giant paper dragons, confetti, and fireworks.

After chatting with Tom by phone after the ceremony to relay the events of the day, he felt better about Mr. Wong and AutoStar. Although we still harbored a healthy degree of skepticism after the funds we sent were used for a purpose other than what we were told, seeing and photographing the

---

[27] This position in China's government, or Politburo, would be comparable in power, prestige, and title to the speaker of the House of Representatives (Nancy Pelosi at the time of this writing in September 2008) in the United States. For further discussion, see the Standing Committee of the National People's Congress at http://en.wikipedia.org/wiki/Standing_Committee_of_the_National_People's_Congress. This page was last accessed on May 1, 2011.

[28] CCTV is an acronym for China Central Television, the national television network of the People's Republic of China. For more information, see its Wikipedia profile page at http://en.wikipedia.org/wiki/China_Central_Television. This page was last accessed on May 1, 2011.

new facilities and passing on the experience of the celebration had helped to set our minds at ease.

Looking back to that trip with the benefit of hindsight, I still marvel at the genius of Mr. Wong's strategy. He knew very well that we would be very upset that he didn't use the $1.2 million to acquire the government facilities as he promised. He also knew that if he didn't have something to show us, the deal could fall apart, and he would never get the remaining $6.2 million. To keep our relationship and the investment alive, Mr. Wong knew he had to show that the money we had wired was being invested into the new centers and that the political clout with high-ranking government officials he had boasted about was real. Although we still had reservations, the fact that we now saw the new centers operational and starting to generate revenue greatly eased our minds. Although the $1.2 million wasn't employed as intended, it apparently was being used to expand current business, and Tom had an income-producing asset to show for his investment. There was still an obligation to contribute the full $8 million to the joint venture. This funding was merely the first installment and went exactly for what was originally planned—the expansion of the AutoStar facilities in Beijing. That was the game plan. Mr. Wong, after all, had contributed nearly $20 million of his company's assets (or so we believed at the time). "Things could be worse," I thought to myself as I gazed down from the plane at the Siberian tundra below on my trip back home. I wondered how much money the amazing events I had just been a part of must have cost Mr. Wong.[29] What I didn't realize at the time was just how much more this adventure was going to cost everyone.

---

[29] Although it would be nearly impossible to prove, I feel quite confident that the expensive signing ceremony (including paying off the government officials to attend) was bought and paid for with ABC Capital's $1.2 million wire transfer. I don't think a dime of that cost was paid for out of Mr. Wong's pocket.

CHAPTER 5 ═══════

Completing the Puzzle

After returning home, and at the direction of Tom and ABC Capital, I began to put into motion the organizational, operational, legal, and financial steps necessary to prepare the AutoStar/Plymouth joint venture to take it public. This was an essential first step to make the joint venture SEC compliant, allowing the legal merger into the shell company and the public listing and trading of the stock.[30]

The first step in accomplishing this task was to restructure and modernize AutoStar's internal accounting and control systems to prepare it for the SEC-mandated GAAP audit. Not only would the audit help us prepare for the merger and listing, we felt it would also allow us to institute better controls and provide greater oversight over our investment in the joint venture. Although AutoStar already had an audit, Tom felt that a GAAP audit, by a firm selected by ABC Capital, would be in everyone's best interest.

---

[30] The United States Securities and Exchange Commission (commonly known as the SEC) is a US government agency having primary responsibility for enforcing the federal securities laws and regulating the securities industry/stock market. The SEC was created by Section 4 of the Securities Exchange Act of 1934 (now codified as 15 U.S.C. § 78d and commonly referred to as the 1934 Act). In addition to the 1934 Act that created it, the SEC enforces the Securities Act of 1933, the Trust Indenture Act of 1939, the Investment Company Act of 1940, the Investment Advisers Act of 1940, the Sarbanes-Oxley Act of 2002, and other statutes. For more information, see the SEC website at http://www.sec.gov/. This page was last accessed on May 1, 2011.

Before hiring an international accounting firm to pore over the books and produce an audit, however, it was felt that the company should do as much of the basic financial restructuring as possible. To do that, the company needed to identify and hire its own chief financial officer (CFO), along with a small staff to support him or her. This team would work with AutoStar's in-house accounting staff to modernize the firm's accounting records and processes. From our perspective, an ideal CFO candidate would be a seasoned professional with extensive experience in detecting and correcting corporate financial problems. At the same time, this person must possess the enormous patience needed for working within the archaic Chinese business environment. Perhaps most importantly, we also needed a veteran executive who would ensure the integrity of ABC Capital's investment—first in the joint venture and later, after completion of the reverse merger and absorption into Deep Doo Doo Inc., in the shell company.

I didn't have to think very hard to come up with my first choice for CFO. My longtime friend Ted Stern was exactly the kind of professional we were looking for. A seasoned and experienced CPA, Ted worked for years at Deloitte & Touché before leaving to manage a corporate investment banking and business consulting firm.[31] I knew that Ted was recently divorced and had two lovely daughters. I figured the fact that Ted was single, and that his daughters were getting older, would make it easier to attract him, since the person we chose would have to spend a great deal of time in Beijing. Perhaps most importantly, Ted was a person of the highest integrity, and I had absolute trust in him.

Prior to speaking with Ted, I discussed his possible hiring with Scott. Scott was the managing member of Plymouth and my close friend. He was a self-made man who ran a very successful construction company in southwest Florida, and he could be counted on for "telling it straight." He

---

[31]   Deloitte Touche Tohmatsu (also referred to as Deloitte & Touché) is one of the largest professional services firms in the world and one of the Big Four accounting firms. The others include PricewaterhouseCoopers, Ernst & Young, and KPMG. See the previous reference to the Big Four for further information.

had been there through most of the discussions with ABC Capital and knew that we now needed a competent CFO if AutoStar was to go public.

However, I knew that Ted & Scott were polar opposites. Scott was a take-charge executive. Tell Scott you want something done, and you never had to ask a second time. Ted was a planner. Tell Ted you wanted to buy a company, and he'd build financial models and know more about the company than their CFO. Each man was competent but very different. Scott wanted to get the CFO in place as badly as Tom. They both wanted to put Ted to work as quickly as possible. AutoStar's accounting department needed a CFO to take charge of the public process. Therefore, Scott scheduled a call with Ted upon my return from China.

The morning after returning from Beijing, Scott and I called Ted, and I made my pitch. During a long conversation, I described virtually every detail about what we were doing and why we needed him. I described how the deal was being structured, who the parties were, and what our objectives were. I carefully reviewed what I saw as the potential of the project as well as the risks involved. I was completely up-front with Ted and didn't mask a single detail. Scott was equally straightforward, adding details to questions from Ted and also asking questions of his own. In the end, Scott gave Ted high marks and felt he should be hired so that he could get started as soon as possible.

However, despite my best efforts, bringing Ted on board didn't happen right away. It took several weeks of discussion and negotiation to land him. Perhaps the biggest hurdle in hiring Ted was the fact that his acceptance would keep him in China for five or six months out of the year. Fortunately, after nearly a month of talks between me, ABC Capital, and Scott, Ted agreed to accept the position. Once he made the decision, it was clear that he was excited about the prospect of working with a fast-growing company in China that would soon enter the public markets. He couldn't wait to start.

About a week later, I took Ted to New York to meet Tom and the other partners at ABC Capital to make sure that everyone was on board with Ted as the joint venture's CFO. Since ABC Capital was solely funding the investment, it obviously was important to get their approval to hire

Ted. Any apprehension I had that ABC Capital might not take a liking to Ted was quickly dispelled at dinner when Tom leaned over to me and said that I had found the perfect guy. I was elated. I would be working with someone I trusted in the most critical position in the company. We had our CFO!

Tom and I both agreed that hiring our own CFO to oversee the joint venture was an absolute prerequisite for ABC Capital to invest another dime in AutoStar. And while Tom and I were happy and felt fortunate to have been able to hire Ted as our CFO, Mr. Wong definitely was not pleased. After returning from New York, I called Mr. Wong and told him of our intention to hire a CFO to oversee the financial aspects of AutoStar's operations. At first, Mr. Wong calmly rejected the idea, saying that his company already was GAAP compliant (although I am sure he had no idea what GAAP was or meant) and that the company operated perfectly as currently managed. I patiently explained to Mr. Wong that AutoStar had no hope of additional funding from ABC Capital unless Tom could put an independent CFO in the company. Going public is a very difficult process, I told him. It would be difficult, if not impossible, for AutoStar to be a public company unless he brought in a seasoned American CFO.

Suddenly, Mr. Wong's disposition dramatically changed. In all the months I'd known him, I had never seen Mr. Wong unhappy or even in a bad mood, let alone angry. But when he realized that he had no choice but to accept this condition for the deal to move forward, I could tell from his tone that he was livid. At that point, Mr. Wong abruptly put an end to the call, telling us that he would have to discuss this matter with his family and senior managers.

Several days later, Mr. Wong scheduled another meeting to discuss the CFO issue. Dispensing with the usual pleasantries to emphasize his displeasure, Mr. Wong flatly stated that since AutoStar already had a capable CFO, if we insisted on bringing in our own outside CFO, we would have to pay him out of our pocket. This brings me to Refkin's Rule #9.

> **Refkin's Rule #9: When putting a business deal together, be prepared to foot the bill.**
>
> When doing business in China, Western businessmen should be prepared to foot the bill. Chinese businessmen will never spend any of their own money if they can help it—they'll spend yours.

Although I was not prepared for Mr. Wong's loss of temper during my first conversation, I wasn't surprised by his refusal to fund Ted's salary and expenses during the second. However, there was still $600,000 from the initial funding to cover expenses related to going public. Everyone knew about it, including Mr. Wong. That's where the funds to pay Ted eventually came from.

Based on extensive experience, I have found Chinese people are exceptionally thrifty—as are the cultures of most other nations with underdeveloped financial systems. Despite China's manufacturing prowess, its capital markets and banking system are primitive compared to those that exist in the United States and Western Europe. Because financing options are so limited for both individuals and business enterprises, the Chinese historically have relied on personal savings to finance everything from business startups and corporate expansion to health care, retirement, and education. In fact, China has one of the highest national savings rates in the world.[32]

Because of China's financial system underdevelopment, the vast majority of transactions in China still are based on cash, and most Chinese businessmen will do whatever they can to get foreigners to foot the bill. In the case of AutoStar, Mr. Wong wanted Tom to provide the financing, not

---

[32]   China's personal savings rate was about 25% and national saving was around 47% in 2005. That compares with 0.5% personal savings and 12% national savings for the United States. For further discussion, see L. Shimek and Y. Wen, "Why Do Chinese Households Save So Much?" *International Economic Trends, Federal Reserve Bank of St. Louis* (2008). http://research.stlouisfed.org/publications /iet/20080801/iet.pdf. This page was last accessed May 1, 2011.

only to fund Ted's position, but to pay for all of the legal and accounting fees necessary to get his company public. His objective was to finance AutoStar's expansion, as well as all of the accounting and legal work, without spending a penny of his own. In the end, through his deception, he was able to do just that by disguising his reasons for asking Tom for financing up front. This was a valuable lesson I learned.

Several weeks later, Ted finally arrived in Beijing. Like everyone I've met who travels to China for the first time, Ted was astonished by the masses of people and the incredible scale of the place. I must admit that I was a bit concerned that, like so many other people who travel to live in a foreign country, Ted would experience *culture shock*.[33] But Ted had no problem at all adjusting to life in China—taking to life in Beijing like a duck takes to water. After living in China for just a short time, Ted even learned to communicate well enough in Mandarin to get around China completely on his own.

Soon after his arrival, Ted assumed his role at AutoStar. Ted's first day on the job was not unlike the first day for any new employee. It was basically a "meet and greet" day in which he was shown to his office and was introduced to Mr. Wong, the members of Mr. Wong's family who were working there, and the rest of the AutoStar staff, including his interpreter.

After that first day, however, Ted wasted no time getting to work. He began by meeting with AutoStar's accountants to review and reorganize the company's books. Even though he had viewed much of the firm's financial data before he arrived, Ted knew that without reviewing the supporting documentation, counting the inventory, or walking through

---

[33]   *Culture shock* is an expression used to describe the anxiety and feelings of surprise, disorientation, and confusion that occur when people have to operate within an entirely different cultural or social environment, such as a foreign country. It grows out of the emotional problems many people experience in assimilating the new culture. For further discussion of culture shock, see its Wikipedia profile at http://en.wikipedia.org/wiki/Culture_shock. This page was last accessed on May 1, 2011.

the facilities, there was no way to vouch for the integrity of the statements he was given. He assumed he had been given an unaudited company and went from there. I was happy to finally have Ted in place. His presence there gave everyone a level of comfort they hadn't had since the beginning of this adventure. They knew the best thing they could do was to let Ted do his thing.

Later that day, I happened to cross paths with Ted as he walked down one of the hallways in AutoStar's headquarter offices and noticed, as he approached, that he was shaking his head and had a familiar sheepish grin on his face. As we met, Ted silently nodded me toward an empty office. We entered, noiselessly closing the door behind us. I couldn't imagine what was on his mind as I grinned and asked him what was up. Ted quietly explained to me that a couple of hours earlier he had slumped into his chair, exhausted from both the jet lag, the intensity of that first day, and his realization of the enormity of the task in front of him. At that moment, he said he jokingly exclaimed in front of his interpreter that he could really use an ice cold beer. "An hour later," Ted whispered to me incredulously, "a guy comes into my office rolling in a refrigerator, followed by another guy lugging two cases of Bud!" Ted said that when he asked his interpreter what was going on, she told him that when he mentioned he could use a beer, she told the office manager to go out and get him some along with a refrigerator to keep it cold. "Amazing!" he said. From that day forward, I know that Ted was much more cognizant about what he said.

As the days passed, and Ted began to collect supporting documentation, collate the data, and generally prepare AutoStar for the looming GAAP audit, he soon realized that he would have to assemble a Western-educated and professionally competent accounting staff. Although the existing AutoStar staff was willing to work hard and often worked late into the night to support his efforts, they didn't possess the education and experience Ted needed to get the job done.

After a relatively short search, Ted was able to identify a firm in Beijing run by a group of American expatriates and former Big Four accounting professionals professionals who decided to strike out on their own. This firm had just what Ted was looking for. The accountants at this firm possessed considerable expertise in bringing the accounting records and systems at Chinese companies into alignment with Western standards to prepare them for American GAAP audits. The firm was run by Jill, a gregarious American in her mid-fifties who had a wonderful sense of humor and a keen business mind. We were all very impressed with Jill's firm, her clientele, and her experience. With Jill's help, Ted was confident he could quickly transform AutoStar's accounting department into one that would be capable of functioning under strict GAAP standards.

Before bringing Jill and her firm into AutoStar's offices, I arranged for a meeting between me, Ted, and Mr. Wong to introduce Jill and her firm. More importantly, I wanted to have the meeting to ensure that Mr. Wong and his staff would fully cooperate with and assist Jill and her associates in their task. Getting Mr. Wong to agree to this meeting was like getting a six-year-old to agree that he needed to go to the dentist. He did everything he could to put off or avoid the issue. In the end, he realized that I would not continue with our relationship unless he complied with my demand. Tom wanted it, and, most importantly, Ted wanted it.

I was finally able to arrange a meeting after several weeks of effort. With his entire family in tow, Mr. Wong made a meeting date at Jill's offices. Jill gave an outstanding presentation in both English and Mandarin, including providing a list of her firm's clients and their contact information and the services they had provided to these clients. As she concluded, Jill offered to assist Mr. Wong in arranging conversations with her clients to emphasize that the quality of their services was second to none.

When Jill finished, she and her staff left the conference room so that we could talk things over. After they left, I asked Mr. Wong what he thought of Jill's firm. In response, with his entire family nodding in agreement as he spoke, Mr. Wong calmly said that AutoStar didn't need to hire these "outsiders," stating that his in-house accounting department was perfectly capable of assisting "Mr. Ted." Just as calmly, Ted said to Mr. Wong that what he said was simply not true, explaining that AutoStar's in-house accounting staff had no idea what GAAP was, let alone how to comply with it. "We absolutely cannot comply with GAAP unless we hire this firm," Ted said flatly.

Despite Ted's insistence, Mr. Wong was adamant, bellowing, "I don't want it!" Feeling frustrated and bullied, I began to fume. Ted couldn't perform the accounting duties by himself. No one could. He needed a jump start to get the company GAAP compliant. I knew very well that if we didn't hire Jill's firm, we could never get AutoStar in shape to pass the audit. Without the audit we couldn't use the reverse merger to take the joint venture public. If we couldn't take the joint venture public, then ABC Capital would never move forward with the investment because of a lack of liquidity. Tom and I both explained this over and over to Mr. Wong and his staff, but he continued to resist. I began to boil, and everyone in the room could sense my growing anger.

At that point I asked everyone but Mr. Wong and our interpreter to leave the room. After the last person left, I closed the door tightly, turned toward Mr. Wong, and, focusing my gaze, hissed that I'd had it with his attitude. "I've invested a lot of my time and ABC Capital has invested its money into this joint venture," I growled. "You understood from the beginning that taking AutoStar public was an absolute precondition for Tom's investment. As I've explained repeatedly, we can't take the company public unless you can pass a GAAP audit, and I know for a fact that the only way to do that is to hire Jill's firm. You can't suddenly change the conditions of your agreement just because you now don't like the terms!" I said, my voice rising in anger. I continued, explaining that his cooperation would benefit him as much as anyone. "As you know, you will wind up owning 67% of the joint venture. The value of your investment in your own company will only increase if we are successful—but to do that, we need your cooperation. In any case," I asked rhetorically, "Do you really think AutoStar can realize its potential without the cash infusion from ABC Capital?" Sensing my ire and resolve, Mr. Wong reluctantly agreed, finally nodding in affirmation. We shook hands and summoned Jill, Ted, and the rest of Mr. Wong's family back into the conference room. Jill's firm would begin its work the following Monday.

As I emphasized earlier in the book with Refkin's Rule #1, the importance of "face" in China cannot be overstated. Knowing this, I called everyone back into the conference room and, in front of everyone at the meeting, I apologized to Mr. Wong for my error in neglecting to provide several facts that were critical to Mr. Wong's ability to make a decision regarding hiring an outside accounting firm. For even greater emphasis, I declared that if I were in Mr. Wong's position, I would not have engaged Jill's firm either. Mr. Wong smiled grimly, and everyone nodded in agreement. Of course, not a single person in that room actually believed what I had said. But that wasn't the issue, and everyone in the room that day understood that. Face was saved, and we were moving forward. Walking out of the room, I smiled to myself. I realized I was beginning to *think* Chinese.

Having settled the accounting and auditing issue, ABC Capital asked me to immediately shift gears and focus on preparing for the reverse merger with Deep Doo Doo Inc. I had to move quickly to ensure that we had taken all necessary steps to merge AutoStar into Deep Doo Doo as soon as the GAAP audit was finished. Unlike the auditing issue, however, working on issues related to US securities markets was familiar territory. To help me with this phase of the project, I turned to my longtime friend Bennett, a partner at a large US securities law firm we'll call Stock Legal. Bennett contacted the shell company owners, Michael and Matthew (M&M), and initiated discussions with them over the terms of the reverse merger. Within just a few days, M&M sent Bennett a term sheet outlining the basic provisions of an agreement.[34]

During my thirty-year career I've had an opportunity to review scores of term sheets for all sorts of business agreements. Still, I was a bit taken aback by the terms M&M delivered to Bennett. For starters, M&M demanded we agree to very lucrative consulting agreements for both of

---

[34]   In a financial context, a *term sheet* is a document that outlines the material terms and conditions of a business agreement. After a term sheet has been "executed," it guides legal counsel in the preparation of a proposed "final agreement." It then guides, but is not necessarily binding, as the signatories negotiate, usually with legal counsel, the final terms of their agreement. The term sheet generally includes the amount of money that will be invested, the schedule of payments, and the value that the investment places on equity shares. Typically, a term sheet is used in the venture capital industry and is prepared by the lead investor. For further discussion and references, see its Wikipedia profile at http://en.wikipedia.org/wiki/Term_sheet. This page was last accessed on May 1, 2011.

them at $145,000 each per year for a five-year period, two years payable in advance to each; $2 million to each in cash and/or a convertible note in satisfaction of those obligations and for future consulting work; and the assumption of nearly $600,000 in Deep Doo Doo's liabilities. I'd never seen a more egregious and self-serving agreement in all my years. The entire agreement for Michael is shown in figure 8 below. Matthew's agreement is essentially the same.

Figure 8

M&M CONSULTING AGREEMENT

    AGREEMENT made as of _____, 2006, by and between Deep Doo Doo, a _____ corporation (hereinafter referred to as the "<u>Company</u>"), having an office at _____ and Michael, with offices at _____ (hereinafter referred to as the "<u>Consultant</u>").

WITNESSETH:

    WHEREAS, prior to the date hereof, the Consultant was employed as the Chief Executive Officer, President and Chief Financial Officer and was a member of the Board of Directors of the Company;

    WHEREAS the Company has entered into a Securities Exchange Agreement (as defined below) whereby it has agreed to exchange certain of its shares for joint venture interests in Sino-Foreign Cooperative Joint Venture, a cooperative joint venture organized under the laws of The People's Republic of China ("<u>Company</u>"), pursuant to the Securities Exchange Agreement;

WHEREAS the Company now desires to engage the services of the Consultant, and the Consultant desires to render such services.

NOW, THEREFORE, in consideration of the premises, the parties agree as follows: Consulting Services. During the term of this Agreement, the Consultant shall provide such advisory and other similar consulting services to the Company to assist it in complying with United States laws and regulations concerning publicly owned companies and advise the Company on corporate financing issues, subject to the terms and conditions hereinafter set forth (the "Services"). The Consultant agrees that he will perform the Services faithfully and to the best of his ability, subject to the general supervision of the Board of Directors of the Company.

Term. The term of the Consultant's engagement hereunder shall commence on Month, day, 2006 (the "Commencement Date") and shall continue for a term of five years, to Month, day, 2011.

COMPENSATION:

In consideration of the services to be rendered by the Consultant hereunder, the Company agrees to pay the Consultant, and the Consultant agrees to accept, a fixed consulting fee of One Hundred and Forty Five Thousand Dollars ($145,000) per annum. On the commencement date, the Consultant shall be paid the first two years of consulting fees due under this Agreement (Two Hundred and Ninety Thousand Dollars ($290,000), which fees shall be deemed fully earned and nonrefundable. The remaining three years consulting fees shall be payable on a monthly basis, commencing Month, day, 2008. The Company recognizes and acknowledges that the Company had certain outstanding obligations to compensate the Consultant under Section 4(f) of the Employment Agreement for arranging and structuring the transactions contemplated by the Securities Exchange Agreement by and among the Company and the joint venture participants named therein (the "JV Participants"), dated as of January [12], 2006 (as amended, the "Securities Exchange Agreement"). In satisfaction of those obligations and compensation for such work and future consulting work, which both parties hereto agree represents fair and reasonable fees for such past, present or future work, the Company agrees to pay the Consultant Two Million Dollars ($2,000,000), to be paid on the Commencement Date in either (i) cash or (ii) if the Board of Directors of the Company determines that the Company does not have the financial resources to pay the Consultant in cash, in the form of a promissory note to be issued by the Company to the Consultant in such form and substance reasonably satisfactory to the Consultant, which promissory note shall be convertible into the Company's Class A Common Stock, no par value per share.

The Company also recognizes and acknowledges that pursuant to Section 4(a) of the Employment Agreement the Company, previously, in satisfaction of accrued salary obligations, issued to the Consultant Five Million One Hundred and Twenty Eight Thousand Four Hundred and Fifty (5,128,450) shares of Common Stock (the "Incentive Plan Shares"). The Company agrees to register the Incentive Plan Shares on Form S-8, at the Company's expense, with the Securities and Exchange Commission (the "SEC") no later than 75 days after the Closing Date (as defined in the Securities Exchange Agreement). If the Company fails to register the Incentive Plan Shares on Form S-8 by the 75th day after the Closing Date, the Company shall pay to the Consultant Five Hundred Thousand Dollars ($500,000) in liquidated damages. To secure the Company's obligation to pay such $500,000, such sum shall be deposited into an escrow account with the Escrow Agent (as defined below) on the Closing Date and released on the 75th day after the Closing Date, either to the Consultant if the Company fails to register the Incentive Plan Shares on Form S-8 by such date or to the Company if such shares are registered on Form S-8 by the 75th day after the Closing Date. The Escrow Agent shall release such funds only upon receipt of a Notice of Release of Escrow Cash, as set forth in the Escrow Agreement (as defined below).

On the Commencement Date, the Company also agrees to pay the Consultant any remaining amounts of (i) accrued salary listed on the Company's balance sheet on the Closing Date and (ii) any additional loans and unpaid amounts owed to the Consultant, as reflected on the Company's balance sheet on the Closing Date, in each case to be paid in either (x) cash or (y) if the Board of Directors of the Company determines that the Company does not have the financial resources to pay the Consultant in cash, in the form of a promissory note to be issued by the Company to the Consultant in such form and substance reasonably satisfactory to the Consultant, which promissory note shall be convertible into x shares of Common Stock.

Whenever any portion of any obligations of the Company to the Consultant, present or future, is satisfied by the Company with one or more convertible promissory notes, such convertible promissory notes shall be convertible into x shares of Common Stock based upon a price equal to 80% of the lowest closing bid price of x shares of Common Stock for issuance upon the conversion of any outstanding obligations of the Company to the Consultant and Michael. Such reserved shares shall be placed in an account at or prior to the Closing Date pursuant to an escrow agreement to be entered into by the Company, the Consultant, Michael, and an escrow agent (the "Escrow Agreement"), to be mutually agreed upon by the Company, the Consultant and Michael (the "Escrow Agent"). Such shares shall be held by the Escrow Agent until the earlier of the issuance of such shares or repayment, in cash, of all outstanding obligations of the Company to the Consultant. The Escrow Agent shall release such shares only upon receipt of a Notice of Release of Escrow Shares, as set forth in the Escrow Agreement. All such shares issued by the Company shall be registered by the Company on Form SB-2, at the Company's expense, with the SEC as promptly as practicable after the Closing Date.

After receiving the proposal, Tom, Bennett, and I all met to discuss the terms. After just a few minutes of discussion, we quickly agreed that recommending the acceptance of this proposal would work against building any form of shareholder value. And even if we did accept M&M's terms, Bennett pointed out that it was very unlikely that such terms would survive the SEC registration process. Something had to be done.

We all agreed that because ABC Capital controlled the money and had the largest financial stake in the success of the project (and also referred Michael and Matthew to AutoStar in the first place), Tom would have the greatest leverage in ameliorating the terms so that this still could work for the company—and for M&M as well. Although we needed a shell company to make this investment work, we didn't *have* to use M&M's shell. As Tom saw it, there weren't a whole lot of other firms lining up behind us to merge with Deep Doo Doo Inc. We had all of the leverage, and that's how Tom approached his telephone call to M&M a few days later. Although I wasn't on the call and don't know what was said, the revised term sheet submitted by M&M several days later was far more reasonable, and from a different universe, than the original. In the end, we agreed to merge the joint venture with Deep Doo Doo in exchange for assuming a designated portion of Deep Doo Doo's liabilities and for providing M&M a quantity of restricted shares in the eventual public entity as compensation.

With the shell company issue largely settled, it was now time to refocus our attention back on the issue of preparing AutoStar for the GAAP audit required for public listing. As Jill and her firm were preparing the company internally for the audit, Ted was tasked with selecting an outside auditor to perform the actual audit required for public listing. While Ted knew a great deal about American auditing firms, he knew nothing about which accounting firms were qualified to perform GAAP audits in China. It was clear, however, that we needed to identify and hire an international accounting firm that was both PCAOB qualified and had an office and experience in auditing mainland Chinese companies.[35]

Ted began his search by trying to get appointments at the Beijing offices of the Big Four accounting firms. After a few phone calls, it quickly

---

[35] The Public Company Accounting Oversight Board (PCAOB) is a private-sector, nonprofit corporation created by the Sarbanes-Oxley Act, a 2002 US federal law created to oversee auditors of public companies. For more information, see the Public Company Accounting Oversight Board website at http://pcaobus.org/Pages /default.aspx. This page was last accessed on May 1, 2011.

became apparent we would have difficulty hiring any of these firms when it took us more than a week just to get an appointment. When Ted was finally able to schedule a meeting, I decided to go along with him. During the meeting, Ted and I immediately sensed we would have little luck. We were a relatively small company, and it was apparent that this firm really didn't want to bother with us. Nevertheless, Ted was persistent in asking how much it would cost for us to employ them to do the audit. Realizing that there was probably no other way to get rid of him, the partner we met with told Ted his firm would charge a flat rate of US $1 million for the work we wanted them to do. We thanked him as the meeting concluded and left. In the elevator on the way out of the building, Ted and I both looked at each other and started to laugh. A million bucks!

On the taxi ride back to my hotel, I suddenly remembered that David, an accountant working for the large auditing firm (we'll call them Global Accounting) employed by one of my other clients, had recently moved from the United States to Hong Kong. I had received an e-mail change of address for him and intended to see him the next time I visited Hong Kong. David was a Chinese American who was born in Hong Kong but grew up and was educated in the United States. David's firm was respected and well managed, and I knew that it was PCAOB qualified. What I didn't know was whether David and his firm were doing audit work in China, or if he simply had come to set up a consulting practice for the firm.

When I got back to my office, I quickly located David's contact information and called him to find out if he was willing and able to assist us. During our conversation, David told me that he had moved to Hong Kong to expand Global Accounting's auditing business to both Hong Kong and Mainland China. My timing couldn't have been better. I told David all about the AutoStar investment and explained why I was calling and asked if he would be interested in taking a look at the company.

Excited about the opportunity and about the prospect of working with me again, David booked his flight to Beijing the next day to meet with Ted and me. During the meeting, Ted explained in detail what we were doing and what the challenges were. After hearing him out, David told us on the spot that Global Accounting could do the job and at a rate that was about 20% of that quoted to us by the Big Four firm we had met with a few days earlier. Needless to say, Ted and I were very pleased and knew that ABC Capital would have no problem working with Global Accounting. Their US offices were already performing audit work for some of ABC Capital's clients.

We now had an outstanding, qualified auditing firm headed by a person of the highest caliber who I knew would work well with Ted and the rest of the AutoStar accounting staff. Now that all of the pieces were in place, I knew it wouldn't be long before we could complete the reverse merger and take the company public.

It was now August of 2006 and more than a year after ABC Capital made its initial $1.2 million investment in AutoStar. At that time, I can remember finally feeling more relaxed about how things were developing. All of the major pieces were in place, and completing the deal seemed only to be a matter of time. Even Tom seemed to become more relaxed. His periodic financial updates from Ted showed a growing company with accelerating revenue. Although the company's earnings still weren't where Tom wanted them to be, he thought that as the accelerated growth leveled out, earnings margins would improve.

It was at that point in time that I was again approached by Mr. Wong's nephew, Mr. Li. Still feeling stung by the last time Mr. Li approached me with a message from his uncle, I was much more guarded than I had been on the first occasion. This time, I was not surprised when Mr. Li told me that *we* had a serious problem and that Mr. Wong needed our help. Alarmed on the inside but calm on the outside, I asked Mr. Li to continue. Diplomatically, Mr. Li explained that Mr. Wong, through circumstances beyond his control, had gotten AutoStar into a difficult financial predicament that required our immediate attention. Narrowing my gaze, I demanded that he elaborate.

As I waited for Mr. Li's account to be translated, it was at this precise moment in time that I first thought of putting the Chinese culture of conducting business into words. As I have previously described, these tenets eventually evolved into two of my Refkin's Rules: Refkin's Rule #5—the boss almost always uses an intermediary—and Refkin's Rule #7—expect short time frames in which to think and act where money is concerned. I smiled sarcastically as Mr. Li explained that AutoStar owed the equivalent of US $1 million in lease payments for the use of the AutoStar headquarters location and three of our largest centers. The money, Mr. Li continued, was due next month, and the company's current cash flow was insufficient to support the payments. He said that Mr. Wong hoped that ABC Capital could quickly wire the funds to AutoStar's bank account so *we* would not be evicted.

As I've written earlier in this story, I really liked Mr. Li. He's an honest and straightforward person who, even to this day, has never lied to me or led me astray. In fact, I still consider him a close friend. Unfortunately, I was finally beginning to realize that Mr. Wong was about as manipulative as they come. He was a master at using people, and he excelled at deftly exploiting any personal bonds and friendships. If, through the course of business, one of his family members or employees developed a personal relationship with anyone on our team, that person was assigned to approach his or her "friend" with something that the family wanted. And that something was almost always money.

Once Mr. Li had finished, I immediately began to consider options and worst-case scenarios. According to the reports provided to us by the in-house AutoStar controller and by Ted, business was booming. Therefore, allowing the leases to lapse would result in the collapse of virtually all of AutoStar's operations, and all of the time and money we had invested in this venture would be lost.

After meeting with Mr. Li, I immediately called Ted and asked him if he knew anything about the overdue rent payments. Ted called me back a few minutes later and told me that his records didn't reveal any such liability. However, Ted quickly added, just because his records didn't indicate a lease obligation, that didn't mean it didn't exist. He pointed out that he still was in the process of reorganizing AutoStar's accounting system and that it was possible that this liability was for some reason unrecorded. "That may be so," I told Ted. "But the thing that keeps nagging me about this is why in the devil is the rent payment so damn large!? Rent payments are normally made monthly, aren't they?" I implored Ted. "If that's true," I pointed out, "then AutoStar's annual rent payment would be $12 million per year! AutoStar's earnings aren't that much! It can't be!"

After our meeting, Ted and AutoStar's in-house controller, Mr. Wu, went to work assembling a paper trail to establish the legitimacy of the lease liabilities. Although it took a little time, they ultimately discovered what amounted to a stunning case of management incompetence resulting from nepotism gone awry. It turns out that Mr. Wong's son-in-law "Bob," acting as a chief negotiator, arranged with four different landlords to have the entire annual rent payment due on exactly the same day. This brings me to Refkin's Rule #10.

> **Refkin's Rule #10: In China, nepotism rules.**
> For Chinese businessmen, family is supremely important. In many Chinese businesses, the boss's wife and adult children often not only have a large stake in ownership but in management as well. If you think your business relationship will trump the Chinese family relationship, you're wrong.

Bob obviously had no sense of how to manage business cash flows. He didn't spread the payments out over months or quarters, and he failed to stagger the payment dates so that they didn't all come due at once. Instead, he negotiated annual payments all with due dates falling on precisely the same date so that it would be easier to remember. Bob was employed in his position solely because he was a member of the family and was someone Mr. Wong could trust implicitly, not because he was qualified or competent. To me, this was either a stunning display of ineptitude, or it could have been that the Wongs simply didn't care when the payments came due or how much they were. After all, in Wong's view, he now had his American partners to foot the bills. It was becoming increasingly clear that he viewed us as an open pocketbook and had no problem placing all financial burdens squarely on our shoulders. Furthermore, the damage caused by this demonstration of incompetence was more severe because Bob failed to give the accounting department a copy of the contracts. Now the payments were late, and it was *our* problem.

Generally speaking, the typical "American approach" (at least when I was a kid) to child rearing focuses on nurturing younger children by teaching them the meaning and value of kindness, responsibility, and hard work, and then sending them off on their own as young adults to make a life for themselves. Sure, mom and dad will be there if needed—and in the early years of young adulthood that seems more often than not.

The American and Chinese approach to child rearing couldn't be more different. Generally speaking, family relationships for the typical Chinese household are stronger and last throughout life—and the bonds usually extend to any family-owned business. For a majority of family-owned and run businesses, the boss's children and grandchildren are associated and are employed by the typical Chinese entrepreneur. Nepotism is common throughout China. Nepotism rules!

In one company that I was working with, five family members were employed and working under their father or father-in-law, the CEO. On some days, the "kids" would show up and work hard; on other days, they wouldn't show up at all. They all had their offices grouped together, and the CEO's eldest son had the title of executive vice president for administrative services. As far as I could tell, his primary job description entailed testing and playing video games, because on the rare occasions that he showed up at the office, that was pretty much all he did—entertainment. He excelled at wining and dining potential clients and business partners, often taking them out to a raucous Karaoke Television (KTV) establishment until the wee hours of the night. However, if you were to ask him what he did to justify his six-figure salary, he'd be pretty hard pressed to come up with an answer. The CEO's two daughters were no different. Both daughters had a young child at home, showed up when they wanted, and attended meetings with various people in the company when they were in the office. His daughters' husbands were also on the payroll, and neither of them did a thing either, as far as I could tell. One of my first recommendations after arriving at the company was to tell the CEO he should cut expenses by firing all of the kids. So do you think he followed my advice? Not a chance.

Getting back to the story, once we had determined that the debt was real, it was time for me to place a call to Tom. To his credit, Tom took the bad news in stride and remained calm, explaining that the really important issue, as far as he was concerned, was getting a handle on AutoStar's accounting and financial management policies so that something like this wouldn't happen again. He also asked for monthly financial statements and cash budgets to keep him fully informed about AutoStar's financial condition.

Ted's next action confirmed my wisdom in hiring him to get AutoStar's financial affairs in order. Ted took full responsibility for resolving the lease problem by immediately requesting to meet individually with each of the landlords. Ted tried his best to get each of the landlords to agree to monthly payment schedules and a deferral of the rent payments until the firm's cash flow could catch up. In the end, Ted was partially successful, negotiating a two-month extension on the payments. However, the landlords all declared they would throw us out after that time if we didn't pay them in full—and Ted believed them. Interestingly, Mr. Wong and his family were conspicuously missing from all of these meetings. To this day, I still don't know if they didn't show because of a loss of face or the fact that they knew we would take care of it.

By this time, in fall 2006, AutoStar was operating three service centers and developing another nine of them in or near Beijing. Most of the new centers under construction were being built in relatively undeveloped areas around the perimeter of the 6th Ring Road, which was just being completed.[36] As a result, all of the new sites required substantial improvements before they could open to the public. The largest center, a seventy-one-thousand-square-foot monster, was just a framework of steel beams when I first toured the facility. Now it was beautifully decorated, and the area around it had sprouted housing and businesses almost overnight. Our landlords would have no problem re-leasing this space if we failed to make our promised payments.

Because ABC Capital already had made a substantial investment in this venture, Tom assigned Mark, an ABC vice president, to interface directly and regularly with Ted. Mark was meticulous in his management of the AutoStar account. He requested, and Ted sent, countless electronic and hard copies of spreadsheets, cash budgets, pro forma financial statements,

---

[36]   The 6th Ring Road (Simplified Chinese: 六环路, Hanyu Pinyin: Liu Huan Lu), which was completed in 2005, is a bypass highway encircling the city of Beijing located approximately 15–20 kilometers (9.3–12.4 miles) from the center of the city. For more about the Ring Roads of Beijing, see the Wikipedia profile page at http://en.wikipedia.org/wiki/Ring_roads_of_Beijing. This page was last accessed on May 1, 2011.

and other documentation such as receipts and invoices that supported those reports.[37] In addition, Mark was responsible for negotiating the terms under which the fund would provide Mr. Wong and AutoStar with an additional $1.5 million to pay the leases.[38] Several months later, after Mark was satisfied that everything was in order, ABC Capital wired the money, and the crisis was avoided. When I called to tell Mr. Wong that we had wired the necessary funds, I received a response from him through my interpreter saying that he wanted to thank me very much and that he greatly appreciated all I had done. He said that he would like to meet with me and thank me properly once he returned from his three-week vacation in the Seychelles with his family. It was Spring Festival, and all of China was at rest.

---

[37] Pro forma financial statements generally refer to projected income statements, balance sheets, and statements of cash flow.

[38] The total amount was $1.5 million rather than the $1 million required to satisfy the lease obligations because the extra $500,000 was required to satisfy the interest not yet paid on the first $1.8 million note, along with a reserve we kept in the United States for salaries and professional expenses.

CHAPTER 6 ═══════

The Shooting Range

By the fall 2006, I was spending more than half of my time in Beijing and was constantly entertaining American business associates and potential investors who traveled to Beijing to look at AutoStar. I was by then fully integrated into the Chinese culture—always mixing business with pleasure. I can't count the number of times Mr. Wong and I hosted business delegation visits to the Forbidden City or the Great Wall of China at Badaling.[39] During the morning of one such visit, Mr. Wong, Scott, and I hosted one of my American business associates on a tour of the Great Wall. After another splendid afternoon lunch, Mr. Wong and I drove him directly to the airport so that he could catch his flight back to the United States. After we dropped him off, Mr. Wong asked me and Scott whether we had any plans for the rest of the day. It was late Sunday afternoon and business was closed for the day, so we told him we really didn't have anything planned. Mr. Wong said a few words in Chinese to our driver (his nephew and my jovial friend), Mr. Li. Interpreting for us, Maria said that Mr. Wong had something special planned for us. Although she didn't

---

[39] For those of you haven't been to Beijing, The Badaling section of the Great Wall of China (simplified Chinese: 八达岭; traditional Chinese: 八達嶺; pinyin: Bādálǐng) is the most visited section of the Great Wall and is located approximately fifty miles northwest of Beijing city within the Beijing municipality. The portion of the wall running through the site was built during the Ming Dynasty, along with a military outpost reflecting the location's strategic importance. For a comprehensive discussion about the Great Wall of China, see its website at http://www.greatwall-of-china.com/. This website was accessed on May 1, 2011.

elaborate, I knew by then that "something special" could mean just about anything in China.

After about a thirty-minute ride into the western mountains outside of Beijing, we pulled up to the gate of a Chinese military base. The fact that this was a military facility was not difficult to distinguish. The two soldiers standing at attention just inside the heavily fortified main gate were wearing the unmistakable uniforms and helmets of the Chinese army. Behind them, flanking each side of the entrance, were two monstrous and menacing Chinese tanks with their cannons leveled in our direction. Just short of the main gate was a small guardhouse. Scott and I glanced nervously at each other as if to say, "What's this about?"

Mr. Wong got out of the car, flashed a card, spoke a few words to the attendant, and then disappeared inside the gate. About five minutes later Mr. Wong walked back out with a distinguished-looking middle-aged man in uniform—an officer of significant merit, judging by the numerous medals and pins adorning his forest green military suit coat. When they got to our car, the expressionless officer got in without speaking or introducing himself and instructed our driver to proceed inside the base. After about a half mile, we stopped briefly at a second interior gate. As our car approached the gate, the guards in attendance saluted and, in one fluid motion, directed us to enter. As we passed through, I could see the look of surprise on the guards' faces when they saw Scott and me (foreigners) sitting in the back seat of a car. Our presence here obviously was very unusual.

After driving deeper into the base for another ten minutes or so, we pulled up to what appeared to be a shooting range. At that moment, a blur of images instantly flashed through my mind as I wondered silently to myself: "Have I been too tough with Mr. Wong?" "Maybe I should ease up a bit and be a little more flexible with him?" "I'm in China in the middle of nowhere, and no one knows where I am!" For the life of me I couldn't think of any good reason to be where I was at that moment.

We all got out of the car and entered an ornate yet sturdy-looking three-story stone building just in front of the shooting range. As we passed through the building's enormous, thick metal doors, we entered a grand, fabulously decorated lobby with marble floors and accent lighting, its walls adorned with elaborate glass display cases containing every sort of weapon imaginable. One case contained a large collection of handguns—American, Russian, Chinese, German—you name it. Detailed information about each pistol was beautifully and precisely labeled in Chinese. Another case was stocked with all varieties of sniper rifles. Still another contained machine guns. One collection contained a combination of guns outfitted with silencers along with others that appeared to be highly modified.

Through Maria, Mr. Wong asked Scott and me to select several of the guns that we would like to test-fire on the gun range. I am sure my expression of both shock and excitement was apparent. The last time I had fired a gun of any type was in the Air Force more than thirty years ago. During my time with the force, I received relatively little training or practice with firing handguns or rifles. I remembered that during the little training I did have, I was not a particularly accurate shot. As a matter of fact, my superiors could be confident that they could reuse almost any target I was taking aim at.

Glancing around the lobby at the hundreds of weapons, I told Mr. Wong and the officer that I really didn't know that much about guns and that I didn't know which one I should choose. I half-jokingly told them that my lack of skill applied equally to all guns. Anticipating my reluctance to choose, Mr. Wong spoke with the officer, who then instructed a soldier standing nearby to bring us the ammunition for an AK-47 and a Russian Takarov. Scott and I would use the same guns. As the guns were being removed from their cases to be cleaned and readied, we headed to the range.

The range consisted of a score of ten-foot-wide stalls, each separated from the other by thick concrete walls. Paper targets dangled from metal wires that extended overhead from the center of each stall to a point several hundred yards in the distance directly in front of us. The firing distance to the target could be adjusted by an instructor, depending on the skill of the shooter and the type of gun employed.

As we waited for the guns and ammunition to arrive, a thought suddenly popped into my mind. Although this facility was apparently managed by the Chinese military, I had no idea what it was used for or who used it. For all I knew, there was a guy from Waziristan in the next concrete cubicle practicing his anti-American assault skills while an overhead NSA satellite snapped our photos. Imagine, Scott and I were shooting military weapons on a Chinese army base on a Sunday afternoon! There was absolutely no good reason to be where I was. As my paranoia continued to mount, the guns and ammunition arrived.

Through Maria, the military instructor carefully explained the operating procedures of each weapon as he loaded them. It was evident in his manner that he was very patient, surely a desirable quality for anyone whose life revolved around firearms. He was a wonderful teacher and an excellent instructor. By the end of our session, I managed to score several excellent shots into each of the targets (one target each for the AK-47 and one for the Takarov), which they presented to me as a souvenir of my Sunday adventure. As we exited the building and strode toward the car, I noticed that Mr. Li was carrying a package wrapped like a gift. I didn't give it much thought until the following day when it was time for us to leave Beijing.

Mr. Wong arrived at my hotel, just after Scott and I checked out, to accompany us on our trip to the airport. In the lobby before we left, Mr. Wong presented me with a gift, which I recognized as the same package I saw Mr. Li carry to the car after our adventure the previous day. Because it is customary for the Chinese to present gifts to departing guests, I thanked him, and, without opening it, I stuck it into my suitcase, and we left.

On most of the trips I had taken to China to that point in time, I usually returned directly to the United States after departing Beijing. On this occasion, however, Scott and I had to attend a meeting in Shenzhen, a massive, gleaming Chinese city on the mainland just across Victoria Harbor from Hong Kong. Mr. Li parked the car in a VIP area at the Beijing airport, and we all headed directly for the domestic departures gate. With Mr. Wong, Mr. Li, and Maria in tow, I stepped up to the ticket counter to check in and check my bags. That day, I had two bags to check and absentmindedly glanced at them as the lovely young ticket agent, with impeccable English, placed them on the conveyor. A baggage clerk standing a few feet behind the counter monitored all baggage as it passed along the belt through an X-ray machine on the way down to be loaded onto the flights.

As Mr. Wong and I were saying our good-byes, I noticed that the baggage clerk suddenly was very animated as she pointed toward the X-ray monitor in front of her. She began talking very loudly, barking into her communications device while motioning for assistance from other nearby airport personnel. I still only absentmindedly noticed the commotion that was beginning to build. Being in China so much now, I was used to witnessing personal conflicts play out publicly . . . at restaurants, at grocery stores, with the taxi driver . . . you name it. This time, however, as we neared the departure gates, we were suddenly surrounded by a half dozen menacing airport security guards, all with guns (holstered) as they motioned for us to stop where we were.

I stood there momentarily bewildered about what was happening. In the past, I had been detained by security several times at the Beijing airport because of a large can of Right Guard deodorant that I used to pack and take along with me in my carry-on bag. Apparently, that particular size, shape, and brand was rare enough in China that security always thought it was suspicious enough to investigate. After the first couple of times, however, I made sure to pack it away in my checked baggage, and I had never been stopped when packing it there. Scott used to give me a hard time about this, and I eventually switched to a solid deodorant. "I must have packed that can again," I thought. I was sure the commotion was about that.

As the throng of armed guards ushered me toward the computer monitor manned by the animated baggage clerk, I regained my composure, confident that I could allay their concern by opening my bag and showing them the Right Guard. When I got to the monitor, however, I nearly went into cardiac arrest. There on the screen was the unmistakable outline of a gun—with three bullets, no less! And then I remembered . . . the gift from Mr. Wong!

With grim expressions, the security guards plopped my bag on an inspection counter. I was speechless as adrenaline coursed through my veins, and my temples throbbed. They unzipped my bag and pulled out the package. Inside was an ornate gun box that I hadn't actually seen before. They carefully opened the box, and there, inside, was a beautiful gold pistol mounted on a glass pedestal with three bullets on magnetic stubs beside it. As my eyes widened and I brought my face to within a foot of the gun, I could see that it was more a sculpture than a gun—a solid piece of metal in a beautiful gold finish carved into the shape of a pistol. Fortunately, Mr. Wong witnessed what was happening, as it was his practice to wait until I cleared security before he left the terminal. As soon as he saw the armed airport security guards surround me, their guns clutched tightly in their hands at their waists, he dashed toward us barking loudly in heated Mandarin. It was obvious that they were intimidated; they began backing up as he moved forward. As the guards came to the same realization, that this was a statue rather than a weapon, they began apologizing to Mr. Wong and backed off. I also began to calm down, knowing that I hadn't done anything illegal. The security personnel quickly repacked the gift and zipped it back into my bag. Through Maria, Mr. Wong apologized, saying he was sorry that his gift had caused such a fuss. Once again, we said our good-byes.

Our flight out of Beijing departed early, at about 6:30 a.m. About three hours later, we landed in Shenzhen, had our meeting, and then I had a friend pick Scott and me up and drive us across Victoria Harbor to Hong Kong International Airport so I could catch my flight back home later that afternoon. Because I was leaving during the Mid-Autumn Festival, China's second most important holiday of the year, the massive airport was packed with holiday travelers.[40]

I arrived at the Northwest Airlines ticket counter about three hours before departure. I was determined to prevent the clamor and near fiasco that had occurred earlier that morning in Beijing, so I told the ticket

---

[40] China's Mid-Autumn Festival (simplified Chinese: 中秋节; traditional Chinese: 中秋節; pinyin: zhōngqiūjié), also known as the Moon Festival, dates back over 3,000 years to China's Zhou Dynasty. The Mid-Autumn Festival is one of China's two most important holidays (the other being the Chinese Lunar New Year). For further discussion of China's Mid-Autumn Festival, see its Wikipedia profile at http://en.wikipedia.org/wiki /Mid-Autumn_Festival. This page was last accessed on May 1, 2011.

agent that I had been given a gift of a model gun, assuring her that it was a solid piece of metal with no working components. I added that the bullets contained no gunpowder and that my gift was completely harmless despite its outward appearance. She thanked me for telling her, adding that a later discovery might have delayed the flight or my passage on it. She asked me to go to a counter a few feet away while she called a police officer over so he could check the "gun" before continuing to check me in.

I wheeled my baggage to the side counter and waited for a police officer to arrive. About twenty minutes later, a Hong Kong police officer the size of an NFL linebacker appeared with a machine gun looped across his massive chest. He was outfitted in a black jumpsuit and flak jacket with multiple military gadgets dangling from his belt. He did not look amused.

As he held the display gun up for inspection, the officer asked me what I could have been thinking in trying to "sneak the gun" onto the flight. Feeling inwardly perturbed at being harassed, I patiently and politely explained to him that I had told the ticket agent about the gift and merely wanted to inform airport personnel so that there would be no misunderstanding that this was a display model and not in fact a gun. After hearing me out, the officer strode the short distance over to the agent, exchanged a few words with her, and then returned and asked me to follow him, closing up my bag and wheeling it behind him. We walked to the nearby airport security office. After we entered, the officer asked me to take a seat, and he started to ask me a number of questions: "Where are you from? What is your business in Hong Kong? Why didn't you fly directly to Hong Kong from Beijing instead of flying to Shenzhen and then driving to Hong Kong?" After about ten minutes of being grilled, the officer must have thought that I was either telling the truth or that I was the dumbest terrorist he had ever spoken with. Whatever he thought, he told me that I could go back to the counter and get my ticket and that he would see to it that my bag was checked onto the flight for me. Scott and I finally boarded our flight and headed home.

Today, two years later, I still have that gun on display in my office. To be honest, I don't particularly like the damned thing. It's a bit gaudy for my taste. Still, it reminds me of the incredible experience I had and the story that goes along with it. I think I'll keep it right where it is.

CHAPTER 7 ═══

Closing the Deal

As the time for taking AutoStar public grew near, it became apparent that Ted needed more help in overhauling the company's books and accounting system to get AutoStar GAAP ready. Ted barely got any sleep. He had to be at the office most of the day and was often speaking or interacting with ABC Capital at night. When he wasn't at the office, almost nothing got done. He needed help. He was being asked to do too many things simultaneously and was burning out.

During this time I was also consulting for a client in Florida and met an accountant named Jonathan Wan. Jonathan was a handsome Chinese American in his late twenties whose family had moved from Hong Kong to the United States when he was just five years old. Jonathan was a graduate of the University of Florida and had majored in accounting. Since graduation he had worked for my client, a public technology company in southwest Florida. I could sense that he was bored in his current job, which offered little opportunity for advancement, and he was ready to leave. Knowing that the stress of the job was getting to Ted, I had been giving a lot of thought to hiring a native Chinese-speaking accountant to assist him. Jonathan seemed like a perfect choice.

I talked the idea over with Tom. He also thought that Ted had too much on his shoulders and that Jonathan would be the perfect choice if he was willing to relocate to Beijing. With Jonathan by his side, Ted would have a GAAP-experienced accountant overseeing the AutoStar accounting department. Jonathan's Mandarin wasn't perfect, but it was good enough to communicate with the accounting staff, Mr. Wong, and vendors. When I approached Jonathan with the idea, he was ecstatic. He readily agreed to go to Beijing to meet Ted and discuss the opportunity. Not only was Jonathan thrilled about the opportunity to have more responsibility and to work with a company that was moving toward a public listing, he was also energized about living in China, a country he hadn't seen since he was boy.

A few weeks later Jonathan traveled with me to China. Ted picked us up at the airport late in the afternoon, and we drove to our hotel. That evening, in typical Chinese style, we celebrated Jonathan's arrival with a lavish feast and so much alcohol that Jonathan doesn't recall a thing from the dinner or the raucous time at the karaoke bar that followed. Because Jonathan's parents were from Hong Kong, he had spoken Cantonese at home since childhood, but he also knew enough Mandarin to get himself around.[41] When it came time for me to leave the karaoke bar, Jonathan opted to stay because he was interested in one of the young ladies there.

As it turned out, Jonathan quickly found the Beijing bars to his liking and wasted no time assimilating into the capital city's nightlife. In the weeks that followed, it became apparent that he would never lack for company on any given evening as long as he lived in Beijing.

The following morning, as I did on most days when I was in Beijing, Maria and I met with Mr. Wong for breakfast at eight o'clock. We usually went over the previous day's business and his plans for the upcoming day. After breakfast, we would generally leave together for AutoStar's headquarters at about 9:00 a.m. and would arrive about fifteen minutes later. Ted usually arrived at the office at about 8:00 a.m. and would prepare to meet with Mr. Wong when he arrived after breakfast. Ted found the morning meetings

---

[41] Cantonese (or Yue, 粵語) is a major Chinese dialect (Mandarin: Guǎngdōng Huà, 廣東) spoken mainly in southern areas of China including most of Guangdong Province, Hong Kong, Macau, and in some parts of Guangxi Province. Although Mandarin is the official language for all of China and Taiwan, Cantonese is the de facto official language of Hong Kong, Macau, Shenzhen, and Guangzhou (Canton). Like other major varieties of Chinese, Cantonese is mutually unintelligible with many other Chinese dialects. For further discussion of the Cantonese dialect, see its Wikipedia profile at http://en.wikipedia.org /wiki/Cantonese. This page was last accessed on May 1, 2011.

an excellent way to focus his strategy at the start of the day as well as an opportunity to prioritize his tasks. As time went on, he expanded these planning sessions to include Jonathan and other senior staff.

When the decision was made to have Jonathan work for Ted, we never considered that his lifestyle might be any different from ours. We were all in our mid- to late fifties, while Jonathan had yet to turn thirty. As it turned out, Jonathan was often just heading out to the bars at about the same time we were tucking ourselves into bed for the night. Because of that, on most mornings when we met, Jonathan literally looked like he had fallen asleep in his clothes and had just woken up. On many occasions, I'm pretty sure that's precisely what he'd done.

I vividly recall Jonathan's second day at the office. It was 10:30 a.m. on a Tuesday, and we had just finished a morning staff meeting. When I walked into the accounting department, I noticed that Jonathan wasn't at his desk. There was a Starbucks in our office building, so I went downstairs and got myself a "regular tall" and returned to Jonathan's office, where I sat down to read the *Wall Street Journal* and enjoy my coffee. A couple of hours later, at about 12:30 p.m., Jonathan came stumbling into his office. I could tell from his bloodshot eyes and disheveled appearance that he had had a little too much fun the night before. He was obviously surprised and a little nervous seeing me sitting there waiting for him at his desk. Without a word or an expression, I picked up my paper and coffee and got up and left. That was the last time Jonathan was ever late for work.

Although it took some time for Jonathan to adjust to a morning schedule, I have to give him credit. No matter what he was up to the night before, and no matter how little sleep he had gotten, he was always at work on time and gave 110% effort to the job. He never let his personal life interfere with his responsibilities at work. In fact, as luck would have it, sometimes Jonathan's personal life and business obligations would converge, as he often assumed the role of official tour guide and social director for company visitors who came to Beijing from the States. Anyone who went out with Jonathan relished the opportunity to do it all over again the next evening, and Jonathan was happy to oblige. He was articulate, knew where to go in Beijing, could speak the language, and was fun to be around. In contrast, going out with me, Scott, or Ted was about as exciting as watching paint dry. We'd normally talk business during dinner and then go back to the hotel for calls to the United States and then catch whatever sleep we could manage. Beijing was one of the most exciting cities in the world, and visitors wanted to get out and experience the city. For that, Jonathan was definitely our go-to guy.

During my association with AutoStar, I always made an effort to introduce processes or technologies that would be both innovative and cutting edge in China, hoping that they might lead to new lines of business and, ultimately, additional revenues and profits. One such technology I encouraged was the Micropaint repair system, an innovative auto body spot repair process that makes it virtually impossible to notice paint repairs on cars.[42] One of the best features of this process is that most paint repairs can be completed in a little over an hour. There was nothing like it in any automotive maintenance and repair facility that we knew about in China, so it immediately would distinguish AutoStar from its competition.

It's worth mentioning that, when given the opportunity, most Chinese would prefer to purchase a Western-manufactured product rather than a Chinese-made product. For anyone who has spent any time in China, the reason is obvious—very few Chinese have faith in the integrity of domestically manufactured products. As a result we felt that we could create a distinct competitive advantage by marketing and incorporating American brand products and services into AutoStar's product line. When I discussed Micropaint with Tom, he was very excited about its potential. However, Tom's enthusiasm paled in comparison to that of Mr. Wong. As soon as I described the Micropaint technology to Mr. Wong, he insisted on having it—"no matter the cost!" He also demanded exclusive distribution rights for Asia and vowed to immediately begin application of the Micropaint technology in each of AutoStar's twelve facilities. Shortly thereafter, it was arranged for a Micropaint training team to travel to China to train AutoStar's painters in how to use their system.

---

[42]   For more on the Micropaint repair system, see http://www.micropaint.net. This website was last accessed on May 1, 2011.

Having spent a number of years working with, and consulting for, scores of different kinds of businesses in cities all over China, I now have a very good sense of the general strengths and limitations of most facets of Chinese business operations. Most importantly, business in China is rapidly and continuously evolving—and in most ways for the better. Managers are smarter and better educated than ever before; laborers are better trained and harder-working than ever before; and technology, manufacturing processes, and quality at most firms are better than ever before.

Just thirty years ago, the typical Chinese CEO was managing a state-owned enterprise (SOE). The SOE was owned by the government and was focused on employing workers and meeting production goals rather than on maximizing profit or shareholder value. They were employed by the state, worked five days a week, rarely worked overtime, and had a job for life with retirement benefits at the end.

In contrast, young Chinese CEOs today are often Western educated, work much harder and longer hours, and are focused on creating wealth for themselves, their firms, and shareholders. They tend to be far more creative and entrepreneurial and to understand more about management and accounting than their older SOE counterparts.

In 1949, after Mao's victory over Nationalists under General Chiang Kai-shek, the communists rose to power, industry was nationalized, and agriculture was collectivized. By 1956 the private sector had been all but eliminated. The state determined the allocation of economic inputs and outputs, and maintained a monopoly over production and distribution. Under the *danwei*[43] system, the government established the "Iron Rice Bowl" of lifetime employment, in which state-owned enterprises provided

---

[43]   A work unit or *danwei* (traditional Chinese: 單位; simplified Chinese: 单位; pinyin: dān wèi) was the name given to state-owned enterprises. For further discussion of the concept of danwei, or work units, see the Wikipedia profile at http://en.wikipedia.org/wiki/Work_unit. This website was last accessed on May 1, 2011.

housing and benefits to employees, and restricted the ability of people to live outside of the system.[44]

In the aftermath of the economic devastation resulting from Mao's Cultural Revolution, which ended with his death in 1976, President Deng Xiaoping launched the "Four Modernizations" reform program in 1978 to stimulate economic growth. The first step was the decollectivization of agriculture. The resulting rural unemployment and disappearance of local-level revenues created the impetus for the rapid development of township and village enterprises (TVEs). By 1990, TVEs accounted for 20% of China's gross output. These enterprises were not state owned but collectively owned under local governments. While not true entrepreneurs, insofar as they were on a contract system, managers of TVEs demonstrated many entrepreneurial characteristics.

During the 1980s, both official and unofficial constraints on private enterprise continued to exist. For example, a law existed that limited employment in a private enterprise to seven people. In addition, business financing was scarce because of very low income and savings levels and because the state-owned banking system lent almost exclusively to SOEs.

By 1987, a change of policy and repeal of employment limitation laws resulted in a surge toward the private sector. The number of private enterprises grew 93% in 1987 alone. In addition, the central government's recognition of the tremendous waste and inefficiency generated by SOEs helped motivate individuals to move into entrepreneurship. Still, until the mid-1990s, few university students were allowed to choose their jobs and were simply assigned to government work units upon graduation.

Since the late 1980s, however, hundreds of inefficient SOEs gradually have been shut down, sold off, or privatized so that today private enterprise in China dominates the economic landscape in terms of both output and employment. In addition, since the early '90s, China's central government

---

[44] Much of this section is excerpted from Debbie Liao and Philip Sohmen's "The Development of Modern Entrepreneurship in China," *Stanford Journal of East Asian Affairs*, Spring 2001, Volume 1.

has sought to stimulate entrepreneurship through the development of high-tech zones, science parks, and business incubators.

In a symbolic shift, the Communist Party in 2002 changed its bylaws to allow entrepreneurs to become party members, which has helped small business flourish in China. By 2002, China had nearly twenty-four million small independent companies—a number that's growing at 15% to 20% annually. Real estate agencies, car repair shops, and many other categories of service businesses are mostly private today. Though virtually nonexistent a few decades ago, small to medium enterprises are responsible for 75% of new jobs.

Because of all of the change that has happened in China, particularly during the past ten years, the first thing I take note of when I visit a potential client is the age of the CEO. If the CEO is forty years old or younger, he's more likely to be entrepreneurial, less likely to have been influenced by the state system, and more likely to have incorporated Western business and accounting practices in his enterprise. If a CEO is approaching fifty years old, he was likely employed by an SOE and learned how to operate under the inefficient state system.

In terms of production line processes, my impression of the average Chinese laborer is that while most are very hard-working, the majority generally lack entrepreneurial skills and abilities. Most line laborers I have witnessed can skillfully perform error-free repetitive routine job tasks. If you ask them to think outside the box to innovate or improve a process, however, you'll often have problems. That pretty much describes the experience we had in teaching and training AutoStar's auto body staff to apply the Micropaint process. Each batch of Micropaint had to be uniquely mixed and prepared for each application. Then, through a series of sophisticated procedures, it could be applied to blend in perfectly with the existing paint surrounding the damaged area. When applied properly, it was virtually impossible to detect the repair. I know this to be true firsthand through lost wagers I'd made with several of my colleagues from Canada who took me through the process.

Unfortunately, teaching our AutoStar service personnel to master the Micropaint process was akin to teaching me to paint like Pablo Picasso. In fact, even after extensive training lasting more than a year, we successfully prepared only a handful of technicians to perform this process well enough to apply it, unsupervised, on a real car.

A second, more fundamental and more troubling, problem in fulfilling the potential of Micropaint rested with the overall management of AutoStar itself. While Mr. Wong and his family might have been long on desire, enthusiasm, and celebration, they were very often short on competence, planning, and execution. Even though the company successfully trained some of its technicians to apply Micropaint, Mr. Wong, his family, and his managers never once considered how to market and sell this service to the end user. Despite months of training and the thousands of dollars invested in the product, and the construction of special enclosures for its application, the inability to include Micropaint in the company's list of client services was a significant setback financially, since AutoStar could have charged more than one hundred dollars for a process that cost only ten dollars to perform. This disastrous episode underscores the importance of Refkin's Rule #11.

Refkin's Rule #11: When doing business in China, leave nothing to chance. When doing business with Chinese businessmen, foreign business partners should never assume anything. Be sure to get all of the details of your contracts translated and signed by people you trust.

Tom, the folks at Micropaint, Ted, and I all assumed that if AutoStar's painters were trained to use the product, they would be capable of competently marketing and selling it to potential customers. Unfortunately, everyone was obviously and painfully wrong in that assumption. To make matters worse, Mr. Wong refused to pay a dime for the roughly $1 million worth of Micropaint product he purchased. Naturally, the folks at Micropaint were livid and pursued payment. Nevertheless, despite investing several months seeking compensation using every method imaginable, Micropaint was unable to collect. Mr. Wong felt that since he made no money from selling the product, he (culturally) was under no obligation to pay for it—and he told me as much.

As a general rule, I've found that Chinese contracts are very difficult to enforce. In the current Chinese legal system, you not only have to get a favorable verdict on your lawsuit but also have to get a judgment for enforcement of that verdict. It's a very time-consuming and costly process. I believe a foreigner can win a judgment, and even get that judgment enforced, but the case had better be worth the time and cost. It's much better to have a contract where both sides benefit and neither wants to break the contract. In that way you'll never get to the courtroom. However, if you think you're going to be able to point to the fine print in the contract and walk away with a verdict, think again. The system is clearly designed to have both parties work out their differences rather than have the court determine the outcome. In other words, it's very Chinese!

If you come to China and assume there's a rule book on how to conduct business, get rid of that notion before the plane lands. Western businessmen should never assume they are participating on a level playing field against their Chinese counterparts—they aren't. Their Chinese competitors understand the *Chinese way* of doing things; inexperienced or naïve Western businessmen really have no chance. As a rule, succeeding in China still depends largely on success at developing and building personal friendships and relationships with people that are politically and financially well connected.

As an example, a couple of years ago I visited a potential client—a large manufacturing company in Shanghai. During my visit, it appeared on the surface that the company was well operated, demonstrated significant current and potential growth, and was very profitable. The firm wanted to expand operations by purchasing and constructing a new facility on a large plot of land directly across the street from the existing plant. An old village, scheduled to be demolished, currently existed on that plot, and several other companies also wanted to acquire it because of its location. As it turned out, the owner of the company I was working with was good friends with the mayor of the village. Because of their friendship, the mayor's friend (my client) ultimately won the bid. In truth, however, the winner of the bid was never in doubt. The personal friendship between the mayor and the owner of the manufacturing plant ensured that. In the United States this would have resulted in a major scandal and endless litigation. In China, however, it was business as usual. The lesson, of course, is that Western businessmen shouldn't assume that something can't be done in China just because it can't be done at home. Unless a foreign businessman has important personal connections, he or she will always be at a disadvantage in China; if he does have those connections, success is almost guaranteed.

As another example, figure 9 illustrates a contract drafted by a government official from a city in China. I found it interesting. In the contract, the official who approached me simply wanted to demonstrate to his superiors that he was able to secure an investment commitment from a foreign business entity. However, you will note in the section highlighted in yellow that the contract is entirely contingent on the timely receipt of funding from us. Since we had no intention of providing funds, the contract was completely meaningless. So often I've met with government officials who want me to sign a contract like this. I tell them that no one could possibly commit to funding a project they knew absolutely nothing about. They all say that it's not a problem and that they didn't expect a funding commitment. They invariably explain that they just want to demonstrate an investment commitment from a foreign entity. In many cases, officials can gain a promotion in exchange for striking an agreement for foreign investment such as this. And even if they don't get promoted, they gain face, even though virtually everyone knows such a contract is nothing more than "window dressing" and more about image than substance.

Figure 9

Sample Investment Promotion Project Confirmation Contract

Party A: (China City Government)
Address:
Legal representative

Project Principal
Party B:
Address:

Legal representative
Project Principal

I. The name and scale of the project invested by Party B

1.1 Name of the project
1.2 Project total investment____RMB construction investment or agricultural base_RMB，____Processing workshop investment RMB, among which investment of fixed assets_RMB
1.3 Project total construction content and scale
1.4 Project economic benefit
1.5 Project location and land use scale
1.6 Project construction time and construction period

II. Party A confirms to Party B that the project Party B invests is investment promotion project of (local China government agency) (China City's foreign promotion bureau) in 2008.

2.1. Party A will send person specially assigned for the task to actively assist and support Party B's completion of application procedures required by law for the construction of the project, in order to positively and actively solve the specific problems and issues during the process and development of the project under the precondition of the money placed from Party B.

2.2. The project will not only enjoy the preferential policies issued from (China City) People's government but also enjoy the favorable policy of investment promotion from (China City) Agricultural Bureau.

2.3. This company will be included in the category of (China City) Agricultural Industrial Structure Adjustment and Industrial Operation Policy, and enjoy relevant industry supporting policy.

2.4. Party A will provide follow-up services to the construction of the project, so that to have Party B enjoy as much convenience as you could in national, provincial, and civic relevant policies.

III. Party B must complete the construction of the project on time.

    3.1. The project of Party B must be a legal institution with relevant registration, license, etc. within (China City).

    3.2. During the project construction of Party B, the project of Party B should go through relevant procedures including land, planning, environment protection, and be in compliance with relevant law.

    3.3. Party B must insure the committed capital must be put in place on time, and the project should be started on time.

IV. Contract effective and liability for breach the contract.

    4.1. The contract will go into effect after confirmation of the capital, equipment or IPR investment of Party B (The contract won't go into effect until (China City) receives confirmation of the capital, equipment or IPR which has been put in place by Party B.)

    4.2. If the capital, equipment or IPR are not put in place by Party B, Party B is deemed to be a waiver, and the contract will be terminated.

    4.3. After signing of the contract, Party B will not be allowed to sign another investment confirmation contract with the third party, especially a third party in (China City) district, otherwise Party A has the right to cancel the contract with no responsibility to Party B, while Party B will bear all the responsibility.

During the summer of 2006, the AutoStar-Plymouth joint venture was proceeding toward its merger with M&M's public shell company, Deep Doo Doo Inc. However, Ted and Jonathan continued to experience problems and resistance from Mr. Wong and his staff in modifying AutoStar's accounting system in preparation for the public listing. AutoStar's financial accounting system still had a Chinese-only interface, making it very challenging for Jonathan, and impossible for Ted, to understand it.

Although the independent auditors were Chinese and could read and understand the system and the company's financial data, Ted *had* to have access to those records in English. After a period of continued insistence, prodding, and nagging from Ted, Mr. Wong promised that the reporting system would be modified to provide complete access in English and that this conversion would be completed no later than the end of September 2006.[45]

At about the same time, just as we were preparing to merge the joint venture into Deep Doo Doo, another *major* crisis reared its head. And when I say *major*, I mean MAJOR! During the course of their audit, David and his team at Global Accounting discovered that AutoStar's total assets were less than $5 million—only about 20% of the $24 million in total assets initially reported by Mr. Wong and his "auditor" about a year earlier! Even more disturbing, AutoStar had virtually no equity, despite reporting nearly $20 million in equity at the time we signed our initial agreements! This was a shock of epic proportions!

This new development really put us at a crossroads. On the one hand, if Tom chose to fold up and walk away from the whole thing, he likely would lose the entire $3.3 million he already had invested, not to mention the countless hours of time and effort. On the other hand, if he chose to proceed with the merger and move forward with the public listing despite AutoStar's obvious lower value, there was a real possibility that he would wind up throwing more good money at a bad investment and lose even more. A third option might be to try to renegotiate new terms before moving forward—in essence, rewriting a whole new set of contracts and filing a myriad of new and revised documents, forms, and applications both in the United States and in China, a truly daunting task.

The choice as to which course of action to take was up to Tom, since ABC Capital was underwriting the investment and providing all of the funding. Looking back, everyone had relied on the numbers given to it by the audit firm. Our law firm had done its due diligence on the accounting

---

[45] The promised delivery of access to the company's financial accounting system in English subsequently was delayed at the end of September 2006. To date, access in English still is unavailable.

firm and the company, their customers, and principals. No red flags were given to ABC Capital, me, or anyone else involved in the project.

After extensive discussions with the law firm and his partners, Tom chose to move forward and proceed with the merger despite the lower valuation. Tom reasoned that, despite everything, recent financial statements compiled by Ted and Jonathan indicated that the company was experiencing considerable growth. No matter what happened before, ABC Capital's only hope of recovering any of its investment, and earning a return, would be to move forward, run a lean operation, and implement stronger internal controls.

So that's what was done. In March 2007, the AutoStar-Plymouth joint venture was merged into Deep Doo Doo Inc. After completion of the exchange transaction, the joint venture participants owned a majority of the outstanding publicly listed shares of Deep Doo Doo. A subsequent conversion of Class B shares (which possessed voting rights at a ratio of 100 to 1) issued in connection with the merger would further increase the joint venture partners' share of ownership in Deep Doo Doo. Five percent of the joint venture was not merged into Deep Doo Doo but was retained by a wholly owned Chinese entity in accordance with Chinese commercial laws and regulations.

CHAPTER 8 ═══════

The Unraveling

Soon after we completed the reverse merger, Mr. Wong began to press me almost daily about when he would receive the remainder of the $8 million of promised registered capital. Although the increased frequency of his requests was unusual, his demand for money was not. In fact, there was rarely a time when I traveled to China that Mr. Wong *didn't* ask for money. By now, I knew his routine. I knew that I usually could count on his request coming a day or two before it was time for me to fly back to the States—giving me little time to react. Not only that, but any request for money usually was bundled with a list of issues or problems that needed immediate attention. They knew very well that if they confronted me with these issues and requests late in my visit, it would be difficult or impossible for me to meet with them and to adequately research and discuss the issue so that I could wrap my arms around it and effectively address it before I left. (Recall Refkin's Rule #7: Expect short time frames in which to think and act where money is concerned.)

In this case, because Mr. Wong's appeals for money were so frequent and insistent, I knew that something more unusual was occurring. Based on my growing experience in China, I sensed that Mr. Wong and his team were signaling that something was seriously wrong. By now, I knew that Mr. Wong would lose face if he told me the problem directly because any problem or error coming from him would reveal his shortcomings. (Recall Refkin's Rule #1: Remember the importance of "face.")

I called Ted and told him I thought something was up, and he quickly agreed that he too sensed that something was seriously wrong. However, because the accounting system still hadn't been converted to English, it was almost impossible for him to identify the problem himself. So Ted called Jonathan, and together they combed through recent financial statements. After several days and considerable study, Ted finally called and told me that he thought he'd discovered the problem. He told me that, although AutoStar was generating substantial revenue and profit on paper, the company was suffering a serious cash flow problem. Further investigation revealed the cause. Apparently, many or most of AutoStar's customers' claims were not being paid by their insurance companies. When I asked Ted how big the problem was, I was stunned by his response. "The uncollected accounts total more than US $3 million!" This was a truly staggering figure for a company the size of AutoStar.

As my heart raced, Ted told me that he wasn't going to waste another second and would immediately investigate further. By now I was much wiser, and I better understood Chinese business customs and culture. We agreed that it would be best if Ted approached Mr. Wong and his team by only generally asking why the firm seemed to be experiencing cash flow problems—without letting on that he already knew the main problem lay in unpaid insurance receivables. Although he knew this was deceptive on his part, this would help him to learn if his "partners" were being honest with him. Unfortunately, as we expected, Mr. Wong and his team misled him, telling Ted that the problem was due to a tax break AutoStar was entitled to but didn't receive. This brings me to Refkin's Rule #12.

> **Refkin's Rule #12: Evasiveness is a culturally acceptable Chinese business tactic—expect it.**
> Chinese businessmen will never directly answer a question where the outcome is not favorable to them. Evasiveness is not only an acceptable but an expected and strategic business tactic. Chinese businessmen want flexibility to achieve a favorable outcome. A direct, unfavorable response will take away that flexibility.

In my view, based on several years of observation and experience, most Chinese people view evasiveness quite differently compared to most Westerners. Although evasiveness by American businessmen certainly is not rare, most Americans would agree that they view this as being less than straightforward, reflecting negatively on a person's character. In contrast, my experience and interaction with most Chinese people suggests that evasiveness is acceptable, as it gives a person flexibility to achieve the desired results. If a Chinese person—through being evasive—can advance his or her position or stature, Chinese society would expect that he or she would do so. The end justifies the means. In fact, if a person did not use this tactic to get ahead, when everyone around him did, that person would be viewed as foolish or stupid.

As an example, during one business trip, my team was visiting a company that asked for our assistance helping it to prepare to go public. Our team began by poring over the firm's financial records to ensure that the firm's financial statements were accurate. As a part of the process, we provided the company's CFO with a list of supporting documentation we needed to verify accuracy. Once we performed this bit of due diligence, we would feel confident that the company would have few problems surviving the required GAAP audit. As part of this process, we asked the CFO to provide us with copies of the firm's bank statements—a fairly standard request. If we were in the States, we could verify information simply by sending a properly executed request to the bank. In China, as with everything else, executing such a request is not so straightforward. Instead, to obtain the bank records, we were required to have an appropriate representative from the company accompany us to the bank so that we could obtain a printed copy of the firm's bank statements. When we approached the company with this simple request, the CFO refused, saying that he was busy at the moment but that he would have someone go to the bank later in the day to get copies for us. Based on my growing China business experience, the CFO's response immediately raised a red flag.

Later that afternoon, one of the CFO's staff members brought us a copy of the company's year-ending bank statement on official bank letterhead. Sure enough, the balance on the bank statement perfectly matched the amount indicated on the company books. When our auditors discovered inconsistencies between the financial statements, bank records, and supporting documentation a short time later, we confronted the company CEO. With very little prodding, the CEO admitted that he had his bank print false statements and balances in order to expedite the audit process. In telling me this, he exhibited absolutely no sign of guilt or shame. He thought that he was helping and saving time by having all the documents match. I'm sure in his mind he thought we were crazy for not accepting what he'd given to us.

As a second example, after working for a year and a half on a funding project with another Chinese company, the CEO called me into his office and, *out of the blue*, informed me that the government changed a regulation governing foreign equity joint ventures and that the effect was that Tom's fund had only three months left to invest its registered capital. Although the GAAP audit was not yet complete and the original joint venture documents didn't specify a time frame to complete the investment, the CEO said that the Chinese government didn't care about that; they now required every joint venture in progress to fully fund their commitments. The failure to do so, the CEO told me, would result in the default of our agreement.

Startled, I asked the CEO to provide me with the name and number of the regulation that had changed. To my amazement, although it was written entirely in Chinese, he gave it to me without hesitation. That day, I passed the information along to Maria and asked her to try to find any information about it for me. After only a few minutes at her laptop, Maria managed to quickly locate the entire document online, and in English. After scanning the regulation for just a few minutes, it quickly became apparent that the regulation the CEO referred to had no such acceleration requirement for registered capital. Apparently, the CEO never thought I would, or could, verify what he told me. He thought I would simply take his word for it. In any event, as soon as I finished reading the regulation myself, I immediately called to confront the CEO with the evidence and demanded to know why he lied to me. The CEO was embarrassed, not because he lied, but because he got caught in the lie—and by a foreigner no less! He sheepishly confessed that he lied because he needed the rest of the money and that he couldn't wait another eighteen months to get it. He needed the cash, and he needed it quickly or his business would likely fail. He said he knew the funding would not be forthcoming unless there was a compelling reason. He didn't feel the least bit embarrassed about lying—only at getting caught. To him, the end (getting the money he needed) justified the means (lying to get it).

This type of behavior is not limited to business. Through his extensive experience as a professor and Fulbright Scholar in China, Dr. Borgia has found that lying and cheating is pervasive among students at Chinese colleges and universities. In fact, in response to security breaches, the Educational Testing Service (ETS) suspended the computer-based Graduate Record Examinations (GRE) in China and reintroduced paper-based versions to try to control pervasive cheating among Chinese students who took the exams.[46]

Turning our attention back to AutoStar, Mr. Wong explained to Ted that since his company imported Micropaint (never mind that they never successfully used it or paid for it) from a foreign (US) company, the company was entitled to a tax break for up to five years. As a result, he continued, AutoStar couldn't process the invoices to the insurance companies, otherwise the company would owe taxes on the income. They needed the tax breaks to offset the taxes.

Actually, part of what Mr. Wong told Ted was true. Special tax breaks and tax credits are indeed common in China. In this case, Mr. Wong was referring to a rule which stipulated that if a Chinese firm imports foreign technology, the government would consider providing that firm with a tax credit to offset its cost. In an effort to appease Ted, Mr. Wong's staff told him that only one more approval was needed to gain the government concession and that it shouldn't take long for the government to grant it. To support their claim, Mr. Wong's staff supplied supporting government paperwork and documentation and even produced a government official who confirmed their story.

It was during this period that I experienced one of the worst episodes of my life. My "dentist story," as I have referred to it in subsequent retellings, began with a minor toothache. Let me begin the story by providing a little bit of context.

---

[46] "GRE Test Change, Why Always Targets at Chinese Students?" *China People Daily*, P.R. China. Wednesday, August 14, 2002. http://english.peopledaily. com.cn/200208/14/eng20020814_101472.shtml. This article was accessed online on August 29, 2008.

Due to the twelve-hour time difference between Beijing and the East Coast of the United States, international business travelers like me have problems adjusting to the change and lose a lot of sleep. When you combine this jet lag with the Chinese tradition of entertaining foreign business guests at lavish dinners that include smoking cigarettes and drinking plenty of alcohol, your body tends to get run-down. I can't tell you how many times I've woken up in my hotel room on the morning after I've returned to China feeling lethargic and run-down, as if I had a light case of the flu. But I'd done it so much and so often, I was fairly used to it. During one of my morning meetings, however, I felt a lot worse than I normally did as one of my molars began to throb. At first, I really didn't think that much about it. "After all," I recall thinking to myself at the time, "I'll be heading back home in just two more days and could have my dentist in Florida take a look at it if it's still bothering me." Unfortunately, as the morning wore on, the pain increasingly intensified. By the time I finished lunch that afternoon, the entire left side of my face was throbbing in severe pain. It hurt so much, I knew there was no way I could survive two days with this much pain. "In fact," I recall thinking, "if this gets any worse, I probably won't make it through the rest of the day!" I needed to see a dentist immediately. The only problem was that I didn't know any dentists in Beijing and didn't know a thing about Chinese dentistry. And it wasn't as if I could whip out the yellow pages or call information to find one—everything was in Chinese! I'd never even seen a sign advertising a Chinese dentist, much less considered using one.

As the pain intensified by the hour, I cancelled the rest of my meetings for that afternoon and returned to my hotel room, where I pressed ice on my cheek and took some aspirin. As I lay on my bed moaning with my eyes squeezed shut in pain, my mind immediately flashed back to the people I had just had lunch with. It occurred to me then that not a single person at that lunch had a Kodak smile. A couple of the people I ate with were missing teeth. The rest of them flashed grins in various shades of amber or stained black from smoking and decay. "Is it because a lot of Chinese people just don't focus on dental hygiene? Or is it difficult to find a decent dentist in China?" I wondered. I didn't have a clue.

The way I saw it, I had to find a dentist in Beijing with some skill or, better yet, education, in Western dental practices. At first, I considered booking a flight to an Asian dental haven such as Hong Kong, Taipei, or Tokyo. Unfortunately, traveling wasn't an option at this point. I was afraid that the pain would become too unbearable during the flight and that the change in air pressure during takeoff and landing would make it worse. I had to stay in Beijing and find a dentist *now!* I was living in a city of sixteen million people and needed to find that needle in the haystack—a dentist with Western education or training—before the infection in my jaw slipped into my bloodstream, resulting in something more serious.

As I do on most occasions when I am in Beijing, at that time I was staying at a Chinese-owned hotel on the west side of the city. I usually stay at Chinese hotels for a number of reasons—but mostly so that I can better understand and appreciate Chinese culture and Chinese everyday life. On the rare occasions I booked a room at the Peninsula or the Grand Hyatt—on the east side of Beijing—I felt like I was in New York or Los Angeles. In those higher-end Western hotels, everything is written in English, and Western guests overwhelmingly outnumber Chinese guests. In contrast, hotels on the west side of Beijing possess a more local ambiance.

On this occasion, however, I wished I had booked a room at the Hyatt because I knew that my best chance of finding a Western-trained dentist was on the east side of Beijing. Normally my assistant and interpreter, Maria, would be with me. All I had to do was ask her to call around and try and find a suitable dentist. I could count on her for that—for anything, really. Unfortunately, on this particular day, Maria was at the American Embassy for her visa interview so that she could travel to the United States and act as an interpreter for a series of business meetings in New York. So on this unfortunate day, I was on my own.

I took a taxi back to my hotel and headed straight for the concierge. No matter how hard I tried to explain my predicament, he simply didn't know English well enough to understand. He looked in horror at my swollen jaw and knew that I was in real pain. After consulting with his colleagues, he came back with ice folded into a towel. The situation continued to go downhill fast. I wasn't going home. I wasn't getting on a plane. My entire face was now pulsating with pain, and I could barely move my jaw. I had to find relief—any relief! And fast!

It was now late in the afternoon, and I was willing to go to any dentist to make the pain go away. Surely I couldn't be the only foreigner to have a dental emergency in China. My problem was not *that* unusual. How did other Western tourists and businessmen find Western-trained dentists in China? Then it hit me. The answer, once I thought through the pain, was in front of me the whole time. Most Westerners stay in Western hotels on the east side. The employees at these more upscale hotels had fluent English-speaking staffs that dealt with Westerners and their problems every single day! The concierge at such a hotel probably kept a list of Western-trained professionals that their guests could make an appointment with for virtually any medical or dental emergency.

With renewed energy and purpose, I quickly tapped a text message to Maria. I briefly explained my predicament and asked her to call my friend Mr. Li and for them both to meet me in the lobby of the Grand Hyatt—arguably the best Western hotel in Beijing—when she was through with her visa interview. I leapt out of the taxi when I arrived at the Hyatt and raced through the lobby straight to the concierge; I anxiously began to babble about what I needed. Mercifully, he stopped me almost immediately, probably because my mouth was now so sore that I could barely open it to speak. In perfectly clear English he told me there was a "Western-style" dental office called Big Smile Dentistry close to the hotel. He quickly phoned the dentist and booked an immediate appointment for me. Without looking, I reached into my pocket and gratefully stuck a wad of Chinese currency into his hands. He called me a cab, and I arrived at the dentist's office five minutes later.

No sooner did I enter the front door when a receptionist took me gently by the arm; the concierge had called ahead to let them know I was on my way. She led me directly to the X-ray room and took a full set of X-rays. She then led me to an examination room, where I slid into a thickly padded dental chair. As I looked around the room, it occurred to me that Big Smile Dentistry was as modern as any dental office in the United States. The office itself was spotless, and the receptionist and other staff wore crisp, clean uniforms—white dresses, white stockings, white shoes, and starched white hats. "The equipment appears to be state of the art. This is not much different than my dental office in Florida," I thought. You could put this office anywhere in the United States and it wouldn't look out of place. The nurse walked in and poked two large medicated swabs into my left cheek. A few moments later, the familiar numbness of Novocain began to take effect. I finally began to relax, and I closed my eyes.

I felt even better a few moments later when Mr. Li and Maria arrived. After receiving my message, they met at the Hyatt and were directed to Big Smile Dentistry by the hotel concierge. After a brief chat, they left for the waiting room and told me they would take me back to the hotel once the procedure was done.

A few minutes later a young and attractive female dentist, and her even younger assistant, entered the room. She introduced herself in very good American-accented English as Dr. Ren. She sat down next to me and for the next fifteen minutes asked me all about my medical and dental history.

Once the dentist completed the paperwork and forms, she immediately got down to business. First, she picked up a long probe (that looked a lot like the one Laurence Olivier used to interrogate Dustin Hoffman in *Marathon Man*) and examined the infected area around my lower left jaw. It couldn't have been difficult to spot since the entire area was inflamed. After probing the problem for a few minutes, she laid down her weapon and grimly announced that I had an abscessed tooth that would continue to worsen unless it was treated immediately. "You won't be able to travel any great distance for at least a week; if you don't take care of this infection right away, it's possible that it could spread throughout your body—possibly even your heart." "This is just great!" I sighed. "Please take care of this now if you can," I pleaded.

The dentist told her assistant to free up the next two hours in her schedule. I closed my eyes, momentarily entering a moderately meditative state to prepare myself psychologically for the procedure that was to follow. When I opened my eyes and turned toward the dentist, the blood drained from my extremities as I gazed upon the image that all dental cowards like me fear—a long and pointed syringe targeted directly toward the inside of my aching lower left jaw. Because of the infection, the pain of the injection was nearly unbearable. However, less than a minute later, the

Novocain began to take effect, and the pain gradually began to subside. Unfortunately, I didn't learn until long after the procedure that day that the nerve-numbing chemicals that are supposed to keep you from feeling the pain often are not completely effective in the presence of a severe infection. In other words, you can't completely mask the pain. You're going to feel it—at least to some degree. That was a fact I wasn't at all aware of until the dentist took her scalpel and cut into my gum. Even though my mouth was partially anesthetized, the intensity of the pain brought tears to my eyes. It was the most horrifying medical experience I had ever endured. Although it seemed like hours, only twenty minutes after she began the procedure, she was done. She treated the affected area, put an ice pack on it, gave me a prescription medication for the infection, and told me to call her if the pain worsened.

I was feeling completely spent, and Mr. Li and Maria carted me back to my hotel so that I could try and get some sleep. After a hot shower, I fell into bed but quickly realized there was no way I was going to sleep. As the Novocain wore off, the pain in my jaw intensified so that it was even worse than before I went to the dentist. In the morning, after tossing and turning all night long, I called Mr. Li and Maria and begged them to rush me back to the dentist. My face was so sore I couldn't suck on a straw without being in agony.

We arrived at the dentist's office just as the receptionist was opening it for the day. If she was surprised to see me come back, she sure didn't show it. She led me to the same operating room I had used the day before and told me I would have to wait a little while for the dentist to arrive. Twenty minutes later Dr. Ren breezed into the room while pulling on a pair of white neoprene gloves. She carefully examined the infected area and after a few moments said that the abscess had worsened overnight (I could have her told *that!*) and that she needed to clean the area again. She also told me that since the infection was so severe and widespread, the injection of Novocain she was about to administer was unlikely to completely mask the pain. "That's something you should have told me yesterday!" I screamed to myself. A moment later, dentist Ren used a long syringe to administer the Novocain to try to numb the area around my abscess. I'm sure my eyes were the size of saucers as she repeatedly stabbed my gums until she was satisfied. Then she waited about ten minutes before going to work on me again with the scalpel. Despite the anesthesia, during the next twenty minutes I could feel each deliberate slice as she probed, drained, cut, and stitched. When she finally finished, she told me with confidence that this time she was sure I would fine. She told me to go back to the hotel and try to get some sleep.

When I walked out of the operating room and into the waiting area, Mr. Li and Maria both looked at me with their mouths agape. Although I hadn't yet seen myself in a mirror, their expressions told me all I needed to know. I was ice cold and shivering uncontrollably as I walked up to the receptionist and paid the bill (together, both visits totaled about one hundred US dollars). I continued to tremble as we stepped outside into the warm sunshine and got into the car. Despite the warmth of the day, I asked Mr. Li to crank the heat all the way up during the short drive back to the hotel. By the time we got there, both Mr. Li and Maria were soaked with sweat, while I continued to shiver in the back seat and all the way up to my room. I was exhausted and knew that I needed to get some sleep, but it was nearly impossible with my throbbing and now baseball-sized jaw. As I crawled into bed and tucked myself in, I tried to be hopeful that my condition would finally improve and that today's visit to the dentist would be my last. Unfortunately, I was wrong.

The next morning, my jaw was even more swollen, only now my neck seemed to be sagging. In a panic, I called Maria and Mr. Li and asked them to immediately come to the hotel so they could rush me back to Big Smile (how ironic). Dr. Ren took me in right away. After a short examination she told me this time that substantial fluid had built up due to the infection and that I immediately needed to have it drained. Since the fluid was gathering in my neck below my jaw, she told me she would need to make a "small" incision at that location that would let the fluid to drain and finally allow me to heal. That was all I needed to hear; it was the last straw; I had had enough! There was no way I was going to allow Dr. Ren to slice into me ever again. If I did, I was sure I wouldn't survive! I knew I was rapidly getting worse. Despite the dentist's efforts, the infection continued to spread, and I felt that my immune system was failing. I told the doctor that what I needed at that point was to check into a hospital to get this taken care of properly. She agreed and gave me the name of a hospital not five minutes away that was established solely for foreigners. She called the hospital and made an immediate appointment with a dentist on their staff and wished me good luck. Her words of attempted comfort only made me angry because it wasn't what I wanted to hear from a medical professional who was supposed to treat me and take care of my problem.

I staggered back to the reception area where Maria and Mr. Li were waiting for me and handed Mr. Li the slip of paper that Dr. Ren had given me with the name and address of the hospital on it. Because I was in no condition to make the ten-minute walk to the hospital, we took a cab, which took nearly thirty minutes because of the heavy Beijing morning rush-hour traffic. The hospital was located across the boulevard from the Grand Hyatt Hotel. While the area surrounding the Hyatt is spectacularly beautiful (sort of a cross between Hollywood's Rodeo Drive and New York's Fifth Avenue) the area surrounding the hospital across the street was more like the Lower East Side of Manhattan. The buildings were old and the area was dirty. The hospital itself was an older ten-story complex whose facade had absorbed enough of the grime, grit, and smog of Beijing to give it a blotchy charcoal appearance. The inside wasn't a whole lot better. The paint was peeling off the walls, and the furniture was old, ragged, and dirty. The hospital's overall appearance didn't engender the confidence I was hoping for.

Mr. Li and Maria literally had to drag me into the building and up to the third floor, where the dental section of the hospital was located. By this time I was ready to throw in the towel and take my chances by boarding the twenty-three hour flight back to Florida. But my good friend Mr. Li, ever patient, told me to just wait a few minutes to meet the dentist and see what he or she had to say. "Don't worry, Mr. Alan, this is the best hospital in all of China," Mr. Li said comfortingly. Anyway, it was already too late to make the flight to Chicago that day. It was leaving in half an hour, and there was no way I could get to the airport on time.

I had heard many stories about the long waits that most Chinese patients endure when seeking medical treatment. That simply wasn't the case for foreign patients, who almost always received preferential treatment. Not even five minutes after I walked through the hospital doors, I was in a dental chair with a Western-trained medical professional. As I sat down in the chair that morning I could barely open my jaws wide enough for the dentist to look inside my mouth. After a just a few minutes, he told me that the fluid that had gathered in my neck would drain naturally but that I needed to treat the infection right away. He said that the infection was rapidly spreading throughout my body; but that if we could treat and cure it quickly, both my tooth and my body would be better in less than a week. He gave me a prescription for a series of antibiotics that I needed to have administered intravenously. He told me that I could purchase the antibiotics at the hospital pharmacy downstairs and that he would set up two IV sessions per day for three days. I was able to schedule the first application immediately after my appointment, and by the end of my second application later that evening, I knew it was working. The doctor was right. By the next day, I felt much better and stronger, and by the end of the third day, the swelling was nearly gone.

I left Beijing two days after the last of the treatments, a week later, and made an appointment with my dentist shortly after my return to Florida. By the time I got back, the swelling was completely gone, and my dentist's only comment was to come back to have my teeth cleaned the following week. I was cured.

If there's anything that I learned from this experience it is that China does have excellent medical care available to foreign visitors. However, if you go to China it is very important that you plan for where and how to access Western medical care if you need it while you're there. Anyway, that's enough about my nightmare in Chinese dentistry. Let me get back now to Mr. Wong and the special tax credits he assured us we would receive.

Another two weeks passed with still no word about whether we had won government approval for the tax credit. Tom and I pressed Mr. Wong and his staff. They responded by telling us that gaining approval would take longer than they first had anticipated. The reason, they said, was that the government official was a woman, and it was difficult for them to use the methods they normally use (gifts, dinners, karaoke, etc.) to hasten the approval process. "Unfortunately, there's no telling now how long the approval process will take," Mr. Wong told me.

Several more weeks passed, and again we pressed Mr. Wong. This time, however, we told Mr. Wong that we had discovered the unpaid insurance receivables and that collecting most or all of what we were owed would easily solve AutoStar's cash flow problem without resorting to outside financing. We told him that more than 30% of the invoices submitted to the insurance companies remained unpaid and that we had to use every means at our disposal to pursue them for payment.

At the direction of Mr. Wong, his staff responded to us that they couldn't rebill the delinquent insurance accounts because the firm had run out of invoices, which only the government can provide (I actually laughed out loud when I heard that one). They told us they had repeatedly contacted the government to plead for additional invoice forms but had thus far failed to receive a response. Without those invoices, they told us, they simply couldn't pursue collection, since they couldn't rebill the accounts.

In the weeks that followed, the astonishing list of excuses continued to expand. Our faith and confidence in the integrity of our partners continued to evaporate. In order to finally resolve the issue, Tom and Ted demanded to speak directly to the delinquent insurance companies. When Mr. Wong sternly responded that he was handling the situation, Tom (and a majority of the firm's board of directors) adamantly countered that his word was no longer believable. When it became clear that we were at a standstill and that neither side would budge, Tom and the board asked me to act as an intermediary to resolve the situation.

Despite my deep distrust of Mr. Wong and his family, I had carefully built an excellent working relationship with him, his family, and his staff during the two years that I had been working on this project. Because of that, I was the one person Mr. Wong might feel comfortable with in negotiating a resolution. Of course, I realized Mr. Wong "trusted" me only because he needed to maintain a good working relationship with ABC Capital, not because he harbored any special feelings toward me. Still, my relationship with Mr. Wong and his family served an important purpose in situations just like this.

When we finally met, Mr. Wong admitted to me that he had a problem with the insurance receivables. The real reason, he told me, was that in China, insurance companies budget for their payables on an annual basis. And because AutoStar had grown so rapidly during the past year from three small auto service centers to twelve (and some of them very large), the funds they budgeted for our account still reflected AutoStar's smaller size. "As a result," said Mr. Wong, "our business volume vastly exceeded the insurance companies' budgeted range of payables due to our rapid expansion, and the insurance companies couldn't increase their allocation to us until they moved into a new budget cycle."

After the meeting with Mr. Wong, I called Ted and asked him to analyze all of the receivables from AutoStar's insurance company customers during the past three years. Disturbingly, he found that almost without exception during the past three years, the four major property and casualty insurers whose customers' cars we repaired had paid in full and on time—until recently. Now, *none* of them was paying. Moreover, Ted found that for two of the insurance companies, the level of our business (and hence their payables) hadn't increased at all, while our business with the other two insurers had increased substantially. Still, none of the four was paying us at all—not a dime. It just didn't make any sense.

Over Mr. Wong's vehement objections, we scheduled a meeting with the two insurers with whom AutoStar had the largest receivables balances outstanding. Although it was extremely difficult to get the insurers' contact information, we finally prevailed and scheduled a meeting at AutoStar's headquarters. Both insurers were in attendance. In addition to Ted, Jonathan, and I, Mr. Wong, his family, and all members of AutoStar's top management team were present. Prior to the meeting, Tom and I had discussed this issue regularly over the phone since the day we discovered that the insurance companies weren't paying their bills. Tom was extremely upset, to say the least. I recall imagining at the time that all Tom must have been thinking about was how in the hell he could get his firm's money out of this horrible mess.

Executives from both insurance companies, each in separate, professionally prepared presentations, provided explanations and documentation that confirmed and supported what Mr. Wong had told us. Through the discussions that followed, both insurers promised that, within a week, they would provide us with payment schedules that detailed how they would pay their obligations in full within six months. Although this certainly was good news and would help to alleviate our cash flow problem, we were furious that Mr. Wong—as president and CEO—hadn't taken care of this issue months ago.

Although the problem posed by the two smaller insurers was not as significant in terms of the value of the receivables owed to us, resolving the difficulty we faced with them was far more complex. Soon after Ted and Jonathan began to investigate more deeply, they discovered that AutoStar had sold policies from the four insurance companies to their own customers. They also discovered that this was not an uncommon practice in the automotive repair business in China. Auto service centers frequently sell auto insurance policies to their customers and collect the premiums on behalf of the insurance companies. They would pass the premiums on to the insurers, who would then pay a commission to the service center. It was convenient for the customer and profitable for both the service center and the insurer.

In the case of AutoStar, however, we learned that rather than forwarding the premiums they collected on behalf of the two smaller insurers, Mr. Wong and his family had instead used this cash to support AutoStar's operating cash requirements. As a result, because Mr. Wong had not forwarded the premiums to those two smaller insurers, they rightfully demanded that we pay the amount we owed them before they would pay their payables to us. Unfortunately, although the value of the payables they owed us was more than double the value of the premiums we owed them, the company didn't have sufficient cash flow to pay them. What was needed, therefore, was an immediate, short-term working capital loan that would be repaid by the insurance receivables as soon as we collected them. I called Tom again and brought him up to speed.

Tom was cornered. He knew that he needed to arrange a line of credit, or ABC Capital's entire investment would be lost. On the other hand, he was rightfully concerned that if he did provide the funds to make good on the premiums, the insurers might choose not to make good on their payables. Tom sent ABC Capital's top associate to China to review all of the financial statements and cash flow schedules with Ted and Jonathan. A week later Tom flew to China himself. It was his first trip back to China in over two years.

When Mr. Wong learned that Tom was coming back to Beijing, he assumed that if he wined and dined him and blew in his ear, all would be forgiven, and Tom would happily present him with a big fat check. He actually believed this. Boy! Was *he* wrong! Tom was not about to go back to ABC Capital's Commitment Committee to request additional funding for AutoStar. He had stuck his neck out a yard for AutoStar and wasn't about to stick it out any further. The only funding he would be willing to secure would be a short-term working capital loan from another financial institution—preferably one in China.

Over the course of several months, Ted spoke to multiple potential funding sources. He got nowhere. By now it became apparent that unless we quickly secured a significant source of funding, AutoStar wouldn't be able to operate much longer. Its vendors already had stopped shipments for lack of payment, employees were quitting or refusing to come to work because they weren't receiving a paycheck, and leased equipment was being attached for lack of payment. The situation was now desperate.

During this period, I received an e-mail from Mr. Wong's nephew, Mr. Li, the one person who did more behind the scenes to help AutoStar's employees than anyone else.

Dear Alan,

I regard the situation as very serious. The workers' emotion is very strong and bad, some are already lost their head, and especially some technicians took the lead in stirring up trouble. Right now the salary problem is pressing for solution, we need to stabilize employees. If there is only $150,000 to $200,000 we can put into the company first, and then will solve the salary problem. We all know who cause this problems, but for the company's future and success, we need you hold out a friendly hand and help us go through the crisis. Is there any other way possible allow the money come faster? I know this cause a lot of inconvenience for you, and you work very hard to help us. Thank you very much. But current situation is very serious.

Mr. Li

Like Mr. Li, whom I believed to be sincere, my heart bled for AutoStar's laborers and technicians. Many of them lived in the countryside and endured long journeys into town every week or came from remote villages in distant provinces for the hope of a better future for themselves and their families. Although hard for the average American to relate to, these workers toiled in this way because the roughly $100 to $150 per month they could earn in Beijing was far more than what they could earn back in their rural villages. For many of these workers, half of what they did earn was salted away and sent back home to support their families. Now that they weren't being paid in full or on time, many of them couldn't afford to pay for food or rent. In some cases, these workers went hungry. In others, they slept in makeshift tents and shacks outside their workplace because they had nowhere else to go.

Although the circumstances and events at that time were challenging and stressful for all of us, it was particularly difficult for Jonathan. While the rest of us could leave China after a couple of intense and demanding weeks of work to return home, Jonathan enjoyed no such respite. He could never escape the demands of vendors and employees or the endless barrage of pleas for money from Mr. Wong and his family. I learned a great deal about Jonathan during this time and developed immense admiration for his dedication, focus, and facility for solving virtually any problem. He was a true professional. Despite his mettle, it was clear that the constant pressure was grinding him down. When I worked with him in the United States he would occasionally enjoy a cigarette after work over a beer or two. During this stressful and rather dramatic period, however, Jonathan practically chain-smoked and looked exhausted. Between his commitment to problem solving at the firm all day and his updating me and Ted all night, Jonathan had little time for sleep. His face looked gaunt, and deep lines and dark circles ringed his eyes.

The e-mail below represents just one example of what Jonathan faced every day at work. The e-mail was from Jonathan to me and Ted in mid-April 2007 updating us about what had occurred the previous day at AutoStar.

Alan and Ted,

I got berated by a group of vendors this afternoon. They threatened to bring all the workers to HQ to stop us from working. I managed to calm them down. Mr. Wong's staff told the vendors I represent the American side over here in China. Wong had signed a letter guaranteeing the vendors payment on 4/1/07. I informed the vendors of our situation. I told them that we were working as fast as we could to provide the funding necessary to alleviate the company's outstanding debt. They told me that they lost all faith in Mr. Wong's word but they believe me and they want me to give them a guarantee of payment by 4/25/07. I told them we expect the money to be in by the end of April, but they cannot wait that long. Their hard and fast date is 4/25/07. I informed them to give me one night to consult with everyone and they agreed. They will be back tomorrow and want me to sign a guarantee for payment on the 4/25/07. I have attached the schedule referencing the vendors that were here.

Jonathan

At around this time, the two larger insurers kept their word and began paying off their payables to us according to the schedule they had provided at our meeting. Although the initial increase in cash flow to AutoStar was relatively small, it appeared as if the insurers would make up their overdue obligations to us during the coming months. The company would pay them back the premiums they owed, over time. The insurance companies would pay the company the payments according to an agreed-to schedule. The cash flow from the insurance companies wasn't enough to sustain normal operations. In fact, it barely repaid vendors who had the company on COD. However, there was at least some cash coming in to the company. Nevertheless, Tom and the rest of us had long ago lost our trust and faith in Mr. Wong because of his repeated deceptions and displays of incompetence (it was difficult for me to know which). As my mother used to say, "Fool me once, shame on you. Fool me twice, shame on me." I've always found it useful to compare *trust* to an elegant porcelain vase. Once it's broken, it can never be repaired to appear quite the same as it was originally. No matter how hard you try or how skilled the craftsman, you will always notice the repair. That proved true for ABC Capital. After the insurance receivables incident, Tom lost what little confidence he still had in Mr. Wong and refused to invest any additional funds in AutoStar. Unfortunately, however, he still was trapped. ABC already had invested over $5 million to this point and, if they didn't secure a short-term cash infusion for AutoStar quickly, they would have to write the entire amount off. On the other hand, if ABC invested an additional $1.5 million to keep AutoStar afloat, they could expect to be repaid by the insurance company receivables. Unfortunately, there were no guarantees. Tom was suspicious and cautious—and had every right to be.

During the five months that we were negotiating the terms of the loan, Mr. Wong's patience began to wane and his behavior grew increasingly irrational and unpredictable. Most of AutoStar's employees hadn't been paid for over three months and were threatening to protest in front of AutoStar's headquarters. Mr. Wong's dishonesty had finally created enough distrust that no one—Chinese or American—believed a word he said. At that point, even if he had told the truth, no one would believe him.

Still, Mr. Wong's Machiavellianism proved formidable as he quickly and skillfully learned to leverage the assets he still possessed against ABC Capital in an effort to obtain more money. Whenever he was angry or frustrated with me, Ted, or Tom, he would unleash his vengeance by halting the audit, which he knew had to be completed or Tom would lose his entire investment. He knew that time was tight and that the audit had to be completed soon. I can't count the number of sleepless nights we endured over this. It was the only card Mr. Wong had, but he played it very well. Although this tactic didn't do anything to help him get his hands on Tom's money, it did cause the company to file its registration documents late with the Securities and Exchange Commission (SEC). I knew from my long experience that the SEC permitted an applicant to file required documentation late only twice. If there was a third time, the violating firm was automatically delisted. Because of Mr. Wong's latest actions, the company was now late a second time. If it happened again, the company would be delisted and go from the OTCBB to the Pink Sheets.[47] This was a result we had to avoid at all costs.

Tom was both angry and worried in equal proportions, since ABC's investment would be primarily repaid in stock—which could wind up being worthless in the end. I was angry because I felt that if Mr. Wong had been honest with us from the beginning, we could have created a successful and profitable business benefiting shareholders and investors on both sides.

As time passed and the cash flow situation at AutoStar continued to deteriorate, Mr. Wong and other members of his family began to badger me with several phone calls daily demanding money. Apparently, they thought that with enough persistence, they could get me to convince Tom to wire the money. Of course, Tom was not about to wire any money that Mr. Wong could lay his hands on at that point. Over time, Mr. Wong seemed to become increasingly delusional. I was told by an insider that he even kept his family members awake all night at his house waiting for word on the wiring of the funds.

Faced with the choice of either writing off this entire investment or providing AutoStar with a short-term working capital loan backed by the insurance receivables, Tom chose the latter. In providing the funds, however, Tom stipulated in writing that (1) ABC Capital would be

---

[47]   To be quoted in the Pink Sheets, companies are not required to fulfill registration requirements (such as filing financial statements) with the SEC. The companies quoted in the Pink Sheets tend to be closely held, extremely small, and thinly traded. In general, firms that trade on the Pink Sheets do not meet the minimum public listing requirements for trading on a stock exchange such as the New York Stock Exchange or NASDAQ. Many of these companies do not file periodic reports or audited financial statements with the SEC, making it very difficult for investors to find reliable, unbiased information about those companies. For these reasons the SEC views companies listed on Pink Sheets as "among the most risky investments." For more information about the OTC Pink Sheets, see http://www.otcmarkets. com/otc-pink/home. This page was last accessed on May 1, 2011.

repaid within six months from the cash flow generated by the insurance receivables in accordance with the insurance company's payment schedule, (2) ABC Capital would receive additional stock purchase warrants, (3) all warrants would be repriced at very low values, and (4) all board of directors members would sign resignation letters that Tom could exercise in the event of default. Although Mr. Wong ultimately agreed to these conditions, negotiating these terms took nearly five months. Tom's thought was that there had been several payments that had already been received by AutoStar in accordance with the insurance payment schedule. These payments were on time, and the amount was in line with the stated payment schedule. If Tom received these payments, ABC Capital would get their money back within a relatively short period from a creditworthy source and, at the same time, get everybody back to work by paying the workers and vendors.

Not long after Tom processed the necessary paperwork, ABC wired $1.5 million into Plymouth's bank account in the United States, and $650,000 of that deposit immediately was transferred to China to pay critical vendor payables and all wages owed to AutoStar's laborers. Ted made sure that Jonathan was present whenever any money exchanged hands, and all cash distributions required his signature. The balance of the cash would be used to pay off other liabilities based on a priority list that Ted and Jonathan were assembling.

Late in the evening on the day after the money was wired, an AutoStar employee with whom I had developed a friendship called to thank me for arranging payment of most of his back salary that day. I was immediately confused because I knew that the cash could not have been disbursed yet because Jonathan hadn't signed the transfer request from the bank. I immediately placed a call to both Ted and Jonathan. Both told me that they had no knowledge of any disbursement. I told Ted to call Mr. Wong the next day to find out what was going on.

Early the following morning, Ted called Mr. Wong. Strangely, Mr. Wong would not accept Ted's phone calls; all other attempts to contact him failed as well. Accompanied by our corporate attorney, Jonathan and Ted immediately went to our bank and demanded immediate access to AutoStar's bank records in order to check the account balance and to obtain a record of recent account activity. In response, the bank manager explained that he could provide access to the account *only* if it was authorized by the CEO (Mr. Wong) or if Ted and Jonathan presented the corporate stamp. When Jonathan responded that he was a (required) cosigner on the account, the bank official repeated his stipulations and continued to deny Ted and Jonathan access to the account records.

It quickly became apparent that Mr. Wong had somehow gotten access to the $650,000 we wired to that account without Jonathan's required co-signature. We were confused about how he could know the money had been wired, however, because Mr. Wong currently did not have access to AutoStar's accounting records, which would have provided him with the information that he would need to know about the amount and the location of the wire transfer. The only way he could have known about the wire transfer was if someone at the bank had tipped him off. Although we have no proof, we are sure that this is precisely what happened and that Wong likely provided a payoff for the tip.

After several days of trying to arrange a meeting with Mr. Wong, Maria finally reached him, and he agreed to sit down with me. We had to gain access to our bank records to know what we had in the bank. Without knowing the account balances, we could not pay our auditors; and without the audit we would again miss our filing date and would be delisted. We had to resolve this issue immediately or everyone (other than Mr. Wong) was going to lose their money.

A few days later, we had the meeting at a neutral location in a private conference room in the Beijing Hotel. Those present at the meeting included Mr. Wong and his entire family, a representative from ABC Capital that Tom had hastily put on a plane, me, Ted, and Jonathan. Our team didn't mince words. Tom's representative from ABC Capital spoke first, immediately demanding that Mr. Wong provide access to the bank accounts and account balances. He also demanded to know how Mr. Wong was able to access the account and withdraw the funds without Jonathan's required co-signature.

For the first time in months, Mr. Wong seemed calm and very much at ease. With a malevolent grin, he coolly refused to answer any questions until he got more money from ABC Capital. "Once you give me the money you owe me," he chided, "I will tell you anything you want to know." The meeting lasted another thirty minutes, but with that response, the brief meeting was essentially over with no resolution. Given the theft that had occurred at the bank, ABC Capital would never invest another penny in this project. To spite us and to demonstrate that he was still in charge, the next day Mr. Wong ordered his staff to halt all work on the audit, making it now impossible for the company to file the 10-K annual report on time. Two years of work suddenly went up in smoke. Deep Doo Doo was delisted a short time later.

With the additional $650,000 in funding and sole access to AutoStar's bank accounts, Mr. Wong and his family regained control of the company and told us that we would have to sue them in a Chinese court, win, and get the judgment enforced in order for us to get anything back. This brings me to Refkin's Rule #13:

> **Refkin's Rule #13: When doing business with a Chinese partner, you have to continually prove your value to the relationship to remain in the deal.** As soon as your Chinese partner knows that no additional money or value will be provided, your leverage in the transaction is gone, and the terms of the partnership will likely change.

Shortly thereafter, Mr. Wong closed all but two centers and started a new company that primarily sold insurance but also did limited automotive repair work—or so we were told. Although the establishment of a competing business was in clear violation of our international joint venture agreement, Mr. Wong could care less. If I had asked him how he could justify what he had done, I imagined that he might have said something like, "This is China! This is *my* country! Go ahead and sue me! Give it your best shot! I could care less! I can move all of the assets around and cause enough confusion so that it will be difficult if not impossible for you to recover anything in the unlikely event that you win in court and can enforce a judgment. I have the money, I have the business, and I control the joint venture. You have nothing!"

CHAPTER 9 ═══════

See You in Court

Following the meeting with Mr. Wong, it was time for our side to regroup and to develop a strategy for moving forward. Despite all of the time and money we had invested in this business relationship, we were definitely getting a divorce.

Tom had, on numerous occasions, received feedback from Vera. We were hoping that she could somehow come up with some legal remedy for what had happened. But that didn't happen. She was a spectator on this ride along with us. The only difference is that she continued to bill for the ride.

Our former "partners" had seized control of AutoStar's operations and assets. Mr. Wong was counting on our inexperience and lack of understanding of Chinese laws, rules, and customs. He was confident that our ignorance about the "Chinese way" of doing business would ensure that we didn't recover a penny of our investment.

Although I hate to admit it to this day—the truth is that Mr. Wong was mostly right. Although we didn't think so at the time, we were the chief residents of Disneyland when we entered this transaction. Our thinking going into the AutoStar investment was, "We're in this together with our Chinese partner. If there's a problem we'll address it together and move forward." *How naïve!* Protecting the investment and managing risk was an essential component of the planning process from day one in China—just as it should be anywhere else in the world. But no one suspected that this Chinese partner, with supposed assets at risk, would be as dishonest and fraudulent as he was.

With perfect hindsight, everyone thought that Global Legal failed to advise us properly and to adequately represent shareholder interests. The documents Global Legal crafted provided ABC Capital with very little latitude in terms of their ability to remove a Chinese partner that was acting in bad faith. We didn't know Chinese law or any of the various legal options available to us, but we weren't expected to. It was Global Legal's role and responsibility to provide adequate representation regarding these issues. In my opinion, they largely failed to do so. While Global Legal should have focused on protecting our interests, it is clear that their main concern was to craft a transaction that was in compliance with Chinese law and that would be approved by the necessary Chinese regulatory authorities. Furthermore, as I mentioned earlier in the story, Global Legal estimated their fees would total approximately $100,000. In the end, however, their billings totaled over $400,000 before Ted finally fired them and hired a replacement. The last straw occurred after Ted invited Global Legal to a large social gathering the company threw for its corporate clients and various government officials. The function was purely social. No business was discussed and a good time was had by all; that is, until Global sent us a bill for $3,000 for the time their attorneys spent at our party. To Global Legal, it apparently didn't matter whether they were poring over a document or drinking a glass of wine—we got billed just the same.

Despite its gleaming modern cities, its massive factories, and its increasingly wealthy and sophisticated urban population, much of China still reflects America's nineteenth century Wild West. In fact, I often (half) jokingly call China "The Wild, Wild East" in conversations with family, friends, and business associates. And the truth is that in many ways, it really and truly is. By Western standards, China's rule of law, its contracts, and its legal system are still in the early stages of development.

I have learned through the AutoStar experience that during business disputes, assets are commonly transferred to other family members who are not involved in the business or are transported to alternative, secret locations, making it difficult or impossible to find them. By the time a plaintiff in a business dispute actually gets his day in a Chinese court, the company's assets have disappeared or are so well hidden it would make a Bahamian lawyer proud. Any Chinese businessman worth his salt knows how to do this and is good at it. And this practice is not limited to business with foreigners; it's a common practice in disputes among Chinese as well. And in AutoStar, it happened to us.

The question for us at that point in time was how we should move forward. Should we file a lawsuit and take Mr. Wong to court? Should we take our complaint to the US government? Should we file a complaint with the Chinese government? After some discussion, we felt that the best first step would be to secure the best legal representation available in China. "We need to find the *biggest and baddest* law firm in China!" exclaimed Jonathan in his quirky American slang.

Unfortunately, we didn't know of any law firm knowledgeable in Chinese law beyond Global Legal—the firm Ted had just decided to terminate. And even if we wanted to use them, Global Legal would not be well suited for the sort of complex litigation we intended to pursue since they specialized primarily in contract law, not litigation. In fact, during several of our past disagreements with AutoStar, Global Legal acted more as peacemaker than as a representative attorney. "Try to be patient; this is China," they would often tell us. Now, however, the time for patience was long past. Mr. Wong controlled the company, the money, and the bank accounts. We controlled nothing. We needed an aggressive attorney that wouldn't hesitate to go for Mr. Wong's jugular. We were mad as hell, and we were going to war.

To help in our search for representation, I called my friend David at Global Accounting, who also happened to be AutoStar's auditor. David had always been a good friend and was a great sounding board, helping me to better understand the inner workings and operational aspects of the company. When I asked David for his advice about which law firm he considered to be the best in Beijing, he didn't hesitate. "Liu & Liu," he replied emphatically. "Liu & Liu is an extremely large law firm. They are widely considered to be the best," said David. David told me that he had worked with Liu & Liu in the past and found them to be smart, effective, and aggressive. Those were qualities the company desperately needed. I relayed this information to Tom and Ted, who were back in the United States. Ted asked me to call them immediately and see if I could meet with them.

I called the Beijing offices of Liu & Liu the next morning. To my great surprise, I was able to book an appointment at their offices that same afternoon with an attorney named Mr. Gao, a partner in Liu & Liu's litigation department, and his assistant, Lilly.

That afternoon, Maria and I took a taxi to Liu & Liu's fabulous offices located in one of Beijing's largest and most beautiful central city office buildings. Always prepared, I crammed my sturdy carry-on travel bag with eight inches of documentation that detailed every aspect of the AutoStar transaction. After brief introductions, we were led to a small conference room, where I laid out what I knew. Mr. Gao and Lilly listened intently as I described the AutoStar saga during the next two hours, stopping only to answer an occasional question.

After finishing, Mr. Gao and Lilly looked at each other knowingly before turning back toward me, saying that my story was anything but unusual in China. "Situations like this are much more common than most foreigners realize," said Mr. Gao. He continued, "You must understand that if you choose to hire us to pursue this, the odds are not good that you will prevail. In addition, if you are fortunate to prove your case and prevail in court, you will still be faced with the significant challenge of having your judgment enforced."

Despite his warnings and words of caution, I told Mr. Gao that I thought everyone was committed to pursuing this action and that I would soon conference him in with Tom and Ted, who would be in charge of coordinating with him on the litigation. ABC Capital wanted Mr. Wong's head on a spit, and they wanted Mr. Gao to put it there. In response, Mr. Gao told me that despite the challenges, he thought we had a good case. Based on our initial discussions, Mr. Gao said that the joint venture shareholders appear to have been defrauded and that Mr. Wong and his family and associates had seriously violated several Chinese laws in the process. He cautioned, however, that the Chinese legal system primarily relied on hard, written evidence rather than on testimony or sworn depositions. As a result, he said we would have to provide his firm with a comprehensive paper trail consisting of all public and private documents written in both English and Chinese for it to be possible to win our case. He said that Liu & Liu would be able to help by tracking down official

Chinese forms, documentation, and licenses Mr. Wong might have filed with Chinese governmental organizations. "But you will have to collect and organize everything else," he told me. Mr. Gao concluded by saying that as long as we understood the challenges and limitations, Liu & Liu was prepared to move forward as our attorney. "I want this guy and his family prosecuted and put in jail!" I fumed. "They took advantage of people of goodwill and stole their money; jail is where they belong!" Mr. Gao smiled slightly, placed his hand lightly on my arm, and, speaking softly, replied that "jail is reserved for the more serious crimes like murder or crimes against the state, not for corporate swindlers. The best you could hope is to recover some of your investment. I encourage you to be satisfied with that."

When I left Liu & Liu, I felt confident. "We have a fighting chance!" I recalled thinking at the time. But I was still angry; Mr. Wong had stolen $6 million of the fund's cash and assets and no one had anything to show for it. "Liu & Liu is a good start, but it's not enough," I thought. I needed to find another way to turn up the pressure on Mr. Wong.

Over the years, I've learned that whenever you do business in China, everything is political. While China's federal government sets overall national goals and policy, provincial, regional, and local governments work with the business community to address issues such as obtaining land for expansion, issuing business licenses, attracting foreign direct investment, and approving and facilitating joint ventures. Without both formal and informal approval from local and regional governmental officials and organizations, it is impossible for virtually any business of significance to survive and prosper. Business owners always want to keep the mayor and other government officials happy and feeling that their company is providing jobs and tax revenue to their city. This brings me to Refkin's Rule #14.

Refkin's Rule #14: When doing business in China, you're always dealing with "the government."
When dealing with medium to large Chinese companies, foreign business partners should always assume they are dealing with the government. The government (local, provincial, national, or all three, depending on size and significance) always is involved in international business partnerships. The challenge for the foreign business partner is to understand how.

For a variety of reasons, maintaining China's rapid rate of economic growth and development arguably is the most important national economic objective of the Chinese central government. Rapid economic growth helps to increase the overall standard of living for China's citizens. Rapid growth also provides jobs for the millions of rural peasants that continuously migrate to China's massive metropolises looking for work and a way to provide a better quality of life for their families.

Because attracting foreign investment, capital, and technology are critical to this growth strategy, I decided that this was a lever I might be able to exploit to put pressure on Mr. Wong. I never believed that the Chinese government would condone what Mr. Wong had done, but I wasn't naïve. The Chinese government (or American government, for that matter) didn't give a damn if we made or lost money. But what Wong had done was bad for business—bad for everybody. If the national and local officials could be made to understand the impact that public knowledge of the AutoStar fraud potentially could have on future foreign investment, the government might step in and force Mr. Wong to return some or all of our capital. "I may have to go to court to get justice," I thought, "but the government has a fast track to the finish line." I thought it was worth a shot.

Although I had over thirty years of experience as a successful financial consultant in the United States, I was particularly naïve in terms of my initial failure to appreciate the centrality and importance of the nexus between business and government in getting things done. I had assumed (incorrectly) that, as in the United States and Western Europe, businesses could make most decisions with little government interference or involvement. Boy, was I ever wrong! In China, the interaction between business and government for any business of significant size is critical, particularly when it involves foreigners.

There are basically two levels of Chinese government involvement: national and provincial/local. The Chinese central government assigns specific officials to oversee and assist companies based on a particular industrial sector. With respect to his or her assigned industry, the official is responsible for attracting and securing foreign direct investment, assisting firms in his assigned industry in identifying foreign joint venture partners and leading those firms through the joint venture creation process, establishing and managing government programs for training and retraining workers, and helping the firms under his oversight to secure special tax breaks and other support and assistance. In sum, the central government plays a very broad role in providing support and assistance to businesses.

In contrast, provincial and local governments generally take a much more "hands-on" approach and typically have far greater influence over, and involvement with, companies within their geographic jurisdictions. The top local official typically is the Communist Party chairman (CPC) for a particular district. He's the senior government official in a city or district and exerts near absolute influence and control over virtually all activities under his jurisdiction. The second most senior local official would be the mayor, who has far more power and influence than his or her counterpart in the United States. For example, a mayor can determine if a company will get a plot of land it may need for expansion, even to the extent of moving a village if necessary.

Getting back to the story, the next day I phoned my friend Mr. Kong ("King," I secretly called him), a high-ranking government official I had met the year before who worked for China's Ministry of Foreign Affairs. I was introduced to Mr. Kong through another Chinese government official who thought that Mr. Kong would be able to refer our investment and consulting group to other Chinese companies that were looking for foreign capital and investment. Mr. Kong had spent about half of his time during the past fifteen years in the United States. He spoke excellent English and was well versed in both cultures. We had become fairly good friends and had gotten to know one another quite well. Mr. Kong seemed to me to be a person of very high integrity, so I thought he would be a good person to consult about how best to understand and navigate the vast Chinese government bureaucracy in search of justice. During our conversation, I briefly described the situation we faced, and he agreed to meet me the next morning to discuss it in greater detail.

The following morning, I met Mr. Kong at his office in a vast government complex near Tiananmen Square. Mr. Kong listened patiently as I relayed the story, interrupting only to ask focused, probing questions. After I had finished, I could sense that Mr. Kong was quite upset by my story. I told him that we intended to pursue this in court and had engaged Liu & Liu as our counsel. However, I told him that I thought his government would be interested in knowing about what had happened, since widespread knowledge of this sort of fraud could discourage other foreign enterprises from investing in China. "I'm sure the Western press would love to get ahold of story like this," I told him.

Mr. Kong asked me if I had filed a complaint with either the US Chamber of Commerce or the US Embassy. I told him that doing that hadn't yet occurred to me, as I was just beginning the legal process, but that it was a great idea and that I would certainly speak with Ted and Tom about pursuing that course of action as well. "I'm sure my government will be outraged about what happened and will deal sternly with their Chinese government counterparts," I told Mr. Kong. (Obviously, I was still wearing my Mickey Mouse ears.) Mr. Kong suggested that I start with my government, and he also provided me with contact information for the president of the US Chamber of Commerce in Beijing, whom he knew.

Because of what happened with AutoStar, it was easy for me at this point to feel that everyone in China was unethical, corrupt, and amoral. But the truth is that I've met so many Chinese people who are straightforward and honest and who have a solid sense of right and wrong. Mr. Kong was one of these people. This man was a busy, senior Chinese government official. AutoStar really wasn't his problem. Still, he took the time to listen to my story and viewed what had happened as an embarrassment to China and its culture. He took this very personally. It was gratifying to know that the Chinese government had a person of Mr. Kong's intellect and integrity representing them. We said our good-byes, and I promised to keep him informed about how our case progressed over time.

That afternoon, I contacted both the US Chamber of Commerce and the US Embassy, and was able to arrange back-to-back meetings at both offices the following day. Mr. Kong provided me with the contact information for the president of the US Chamber of Commerce in Beijing, but I didn't know who to call at the US Embassy. So I called the embassy switchboard, like any *average Joe,* and provided the operator with a general description of my problem. Once he had heard enough to make a judgment, he immediately transferred me to the appropriate section of the embassy. After briefly describing my problem to a representative at that section, an appointment was set, and I was told that my meeting was arranged for the following afternoon and would include representatives of two other sections that might have an interest in this kind of issue.

The next morning, I arrived for my first meeting with the president of the US Chamber. I had only a vague notion of what to expect when I stepped out of the taxi and entered the building. I suppose I expected to see a roomful of American expatriates helping US companies do business in China by answering questions and solving problems. What I found instead was an entire floor of a building full of *Chinese* employees working with American businesses. The place was really buzzing. Everyone was busy, and it seemed things were happening.

Soon after registering, I was escorted to a small conference room, where I would wait for the meeting. A few minutes later the president of the chamber walked in and introduced himself. He was very formal and gracious and told me he wanted to hear all about the problems that I had reported to his staff over the phone the day before. He invited me to a small club on the top floor of the building, where we could relax and speak in private.

After we sat down and got comfortable, I spent close to an hour relating the entire AutoStar story from beginning to end as I already had done for many others so many times before. After I had finished, like attorney Gao from Liu & Liu, the chamber president simply nodded and told me that my story was very much like many others he had been told by other

American businessmen over the years. "In fact," he said, "this sort of thing isn't uncommon at all in China. Unfortunately," he continued, "there isn't a lot we can do to help you. The chamber is focused on developing and promoting trade and on making sure that American companies are treated fairly in selling and distributing their products in China. Your situation is really outside the scope of activities of the US Chamber of Commerce in Beijing."

Although he said he couldn't help us directly, the chamber president did recommend that we take our story to the press. "The Chinese government is extremely sensitive about its image, and it would not want a story like this to be widely publicized." He suggested I contact Reuters, the *Wall Street Journal*, and other Western news outlets to get our story out. He also suggested that I purchase a Chamber Membership Directory, which contained the Beijing office contact information for these organizations. A hundred bucks later, I left the chamber with the membership book tucked under my arm.

After stopping for lunch, I hopped into a taxi and sped directly to my appointment at the US Embassy that afternoon. The section where my meeting was held was not at the large compound the Western press frequently reports from in the news, but at an office suite located in a high-rise several miles from the main embassy complex. To prepare for this meeting, I compiled a detailed summary of events significantly related to the investment and ensuing fraud. I produced several copies of the summary for anyone who might be in attendance at the meeting and was prepared for any question that might be asked. I was sure that embassy officials would be concerned about what had occurred and would aid me in seeking redress. Unfortunately (for both me and our government), the meeting was not at all as I had expected or had prepared for. When I arrived at the appointed time I was told that all of the officials I would be meeting with were currently in another meeting and that I would have to wait for a considerable length of time or reschedule for another day, if waiting wasn't convenient. Viewing this meeting as too important to put off, I told the receptionist that I would wait until they were through. The receptionist then directed me to a small conference room behind her desk, where I waited. About an hour later (not at all a long wait by Chinese standards), three consular officers entered the room. They introduced themselves and told me that they were from two different sections of the embassy and were there to hear my story. I handed each of them a copy of the summary I had prepared and spent the next hour reviewing the case. I told them that, although Ted and Tom were the leads on this, I was elected to start the process since I was currently in China. They all were attentive as I detailed what had happened, including what we were seeking in terms of redress. At the time, I'm sure that to them I seemed animated and excited, because I was sure I had found the allies I needed to correct this inequity. "The might of the United States government will be on my side! Perhaps the ambassador himself will get involved," I thought naïvely. Looking back, I realize that I was not only a dues-paying member but the very president of the Mickey Mouse Club!

Exhaling forcefully as he leaned back against his chair, the senior official sighed and said that they had heard stories a lot like mine many times before. "Believe it or not, stories like yours are not at all unusual in China," he stated admonishingly. Although he was polite, the meaning of his condescending tone and response was immediately clear. Not only was the embassy not going to assist me, they were subtly scolding me for allowing myself to be deceived and for bothering them with my complaint. I was listening to the president of the chamber all over again, except in this case, I felt as if I was being a nuisance! Feeling a bit perturbed, I sarcastically questioned, "Am I the only American businessman that doesn't know that fraud and expropriation of assets are common in China!? And if situations like mine are so common, why aren't you guys doing something about it? Why aren't you doing more to inform and protect Americans doing business here? Why don't you put pressure on the Chinese government to prosecute people like Mr. Wong?"

The official's response was very upfront and direct. "To be quite honest, Mr. Refkin, we're more focused on inequities in overall trade and in maintaining a level playing field for American companies that would like to market their products and services in China." In gentler terms, what he really was telling me was, "Look, you're not Boeing or Microsoft. It appears that you made some mistakes and that you were the victim of a fraud. But you're small potatoes, and you're on your own. We're not going to contact the Chinese government about your case. We're not going to make a phone call, write a letter, or file a protest. We're not going to investigate. Hire an attorney; take Wong to court, and good luck. We hope you win."

So that's what I did. I left the embassy that day and never wasted another minute of my time with them. During the next few months I helped Ted and Tom gather documents for Mr. Gao at Liu & Liu. During the same period, Liu & Liu was able to locate and obtain copies of the official documents that Mr. Wong and his staff filed with the Chinese government. The documents Liu & Liu found were stunning—even to me and even after all that had happened. After translating them from Chinese into English so that we could all read them, Mr. Gao explained that the documents Mr. Wong filed with the government were materially different than the English version of the same documents we had signed and I had assumed had been filed. Mr. Gao emphasized that the documents Mr. Wong filed with the government gave complete control of the joint venture to Mr. Wong. Furthermore, these documents stipulated that only a *unanimous vote of all members* of the board of directors of the joint venture could remove the CEO. Since that vote would include the CEO as well as several of Mr. Wong's family members, Mr. Wong had absolute control despite the fact that 95% of the shares were owned by the outside shareholders of the public company. Since Mr. Wong's versions of the documents were the ones filed with the Chinese government, his documents were viewed as the official documents governing the joint venture in China. Mr. Gao explained that unless we could prove that Mr. Wong's version of the documents were forgeries, we certainly would not prevail in a Chinese court.

"How could this be?" I implored Mr. Gao. "We were very careful to employ reliable and trustworthy interpreters and bicultural legal representation, any of whom would have been able to discern any significant differences between the English and Chinese versions of the official documentation." Just as I finished getting those words out of my mouth, like a bolt of lightning surging through my body, I realized what Mr. Wong had done. After each ceremony or business meeting, where signatures on official documents were required, Vera had left it to Mr. Wong to coordinate with her office and to file the papers with the appropriate government department or agency. After all, he was the CEO. However, instead of filing the actual documents, after each meeting where signatures were required, we speculated that he secretly drafted a separate set of documents that granted him full and complete authority over the business, then forged our signatures and filed them with the government. Who was to know? The fraud he apparently perpetrated on us obviously was well thought-out in advance. It was a diabolical Machiavellian conspiracy hatched to scam a group of naïve American businessmen out of millions of dollars. And it worked like a charm. This brings me to the last of my rules—Refkin's Rule #15.

> **Refkin's Rule #15: When doing business in China, expect that contracts and agreements are only a start.** If you think you're going to do business with the Chinese on the strength of the deal alone, you're wrong. Winning a bid or inking a deal doesn't mean you've succeeded or hit a home run; it simply means that you've gotten to first base. Once the contract has been signed and the ceremony is over, make sure your attorney directly files any relevant paperwork, rather than relying on your partner to do so.

To prevail in court, Mr. Gao explained that our fundamental obligation was to prove that the documents that were filed with the Chinese government were not the originals but were forgeries. "This will be very difficult to prove," declared Mr. Gao.

To set our lawsuit into motion, Liu & Liu drew up three statements of claims (lawsuits) against Mr. Wong. The first statement of claims was developed to force Mr. Wong to produce the financial statements and bank account statements we previously had requested and were denied. We also hoped that this first statement of claims would help us trace the movement of the funds Tom invested. For example, Ted wanted to know what other bank accounts Mr. Wong had, what other businesses he owned, and how much, if any, of our investment was left.

The second statement of claims was developed to prove that Mr. Wong had forged the documents he had filed with the government. Proving this would invalidate all of the agreements we had signed and would allow us to pursue Mr. Wong personally, which would make it easier to enforce a judgment.

Finally, the third statement of claims was developed in order to try to recover ABC Capital's invested funds and to prove that Mr. Wong also started a competing business, which clearly was in violation of the joint venture agreement.

For those of you who might enjoy the detail, a summary statement of claims is provided in figure 10. Prior to filing the lawsuit (statements of claims), Liu & Liu sent two letters to Mr. Wong, each approximately a month apart. Each letter formally requested that Mr. Wong conform to Chinese corporate law by providing us with all original documentation, including the articles of association, resolutions of the meetings of the board of directors, financial statements, and accounting ledgers. According to Chinese statutes, each shareholder is entitled to a copy of resolutions of the board of directors, the articles of association, minutes of all shareholder meetings, financial statements, and the right to view the financial ledgers of the company. While everyone knew very well that Mr. Wong wouldn't give us the documents, it was necessary to formally request them to demonstrate that we made a good-faith effort to resolve the dispute prior to filing a lawsuit.

Figure 10

Summary of Statements of Claims (Lawsuits)

A. First Statement of Claims
Plaintiff: _____
Defendant: _____
Plaintiff _____., complaining of the above-named Defendant, alleges upon the following fact and belief.

1. Plaintiff Holds 95% of the Shares of the Defendant.

    a. Defendant is a Sino-Foreign Cooperative Joint Venture formed by Sino-US Yunnan Auto Technological Services Limited ("Defendant"), Plymouth ("Plaintiff"), (Evidence 1: Business License).

---

b. According to the Cooperative Joint Venture Contract (Evidence 2) among the above three shareholders, the respective portion of shares owned by each of them is: Defendant: 62.75%, Plaintiff: 27.25 and Ken Li: 5%.

c. On Month, Day, 2005, Plaintiff became one of the two shareholders of Defendant by taking all the shares held by Plymouth and Ken Li and part of the shares held by Sino-US Yunnan Auto Technological Services Limited through three Share Transfer Agreements (Evidence 3, 4, and 5). After these transactions, Plaintiff holds 95% of the shares of Defendant, and Sino-US Yunnan Auto Technological Services Limited holds 5% of the shares of Defendant.

d. On Month, Day, 2005, the Administrative Committee of (Government Agency) ("GOVT") approved the share transfer transactions described in paragraph 3 (Evidence 6: Approval issued by GOVT). On Month, Day, 2006, the (Government Agency) ("GOVT2") accepted Defendant's application to amend the registration of shareholders (Evidence 7: Approval of Amendment to the Registration issued by GOVT2), and Defendant obtained the amended Business License (Evidence 8). After that, there are two shareholders of Defendant. One is Plaintiff which holds 95% of the shares of Defendant, and the other is Sino-US Yunnan Auto Technological Services Limited which holds 5%.

2. Plaintiff is entitled to Review the Financial Statements of the Defendant.

a. Article 34 of the Company Law of People's Republic of China provides: "Each shareholder shall be entitled to review and copy the articles of association, minutes of the shareholders' meetings, resolutions of the meetings of the board of directors, resolutions of the meetings of the board of supervisors, as well as financial statements. Each shareholder may request to review the account books of the company. Where a shareholder requests to review the account books of the company, the shareholder shall submit a written request, which shall state its motives. If the company, on the basis of any justifiable reason, considers that the shareholder's requests to review the account books is for any improper purpose and may impair the legitimate interests of the company, it may reject such request and shall, within fifteen (15) days after the shareholder submits a written request, give the shareholder a written reply, which shall include an explanation for the rejection. If the company rejects the request of any shareholder to review the account books, the shareholder may plead the people's court to demand the company to provide the same for its reviewing."

b. Article 6 of the Regulations on Financial statements of Enterprise provides: "The financial statements include annual, semi-annual, quarterly, and monthly financial statements."

c. According to the above provisions, a shareholder of a company is entitled to review and copy the articles of association, minutes of the shareholders' meetings, resolutions of the meetings of the board of directors, resolutions of the meetings of the board of supervisors, as well as all kinds of financial statements, and the shareholder also has the right to review the account books of the company.

3. Defendant Used to Provide Plaintiff with Financial Materials Before Month, Day, 2007

a. Plaintiff is a public company in the US stock market, and is required to submit the quarterly financial statements to the US Securities and Exchange Commission ("SEC") (Evidence 9: Legal opinion to be rendered by US lawyers). As a matter of fact, Plaintiff holds 95% of the shares of Defendant, which is the only operating entity invested by Plaintiff (Evidence 10: Investment structure of Plaintiff) and the only source of Plaintiff's revenue. Therefore, the data and information contained in the financial statements required by the SEC are totally determined by the financial report and backup financial materials provided by Defendant, without which it is impossible for Plaintiff to prepare and submit the financial statements to the SEC.

b. Consequently, after Plaintiff acquired 95% of the shares of Defendant in January 2006 Defendant used to provide its quarterly financial statements, bank statements and other financial materials to Plaintiff so that Plaintiff can prepare and submit its own quarterly financial statements to the SEC (Evidence 11: Affidavits and relevant correspondence). Actually, from the beginning of 2006 to June 2007, Defendant had provided its [bank statements, trial balances . . .] and other financial materials to Global Accounting ("Auditor"), the auditor retained by Plaintiff who had reviewed those financial materials on behalf of Plaintiff (Evidence 12: Affidavits and correspondence).

4. Defendant Refuses to Provide Plaintiff with its Financial Materials

a. According to the schedule to prepare the quarterly financial statement to the SEC, Defendant should have provided its financial materials of the second quarter of 2007 to Plaintiff on Month, Day, 2007 However, despite repeated requests by Plaintiff (Evidence 13: relevant correspondence) Defendant has refused to subject financial materials to Plaintiff or the auditor retained by Plaintiff (Evidence 14: relevant correspondence), and had expelled the financial controller appointed by Plaintiff to Defendant.

b. On Month, Day, 2007, Plaintiff has sent a written request to Defendant by e-mail, fax, and FedEx, asking to review and copy its original Articles of Association, resolutions of the board of directors, financial statements, and original account records (Evidence 15: relevant e-mail, fax, and letter to be prepared and sent). Defendant rejected the request without any explanation (Evidence 16: the response of Defendant to the above request).

5. WHEREFORE, Plaintiff pays judgment against Defendant as follows:

a. For providing (1) the original Articles of Association, all resolutions of the board of directors of Defendant, financial statements to

Plaintiff so that Plaintiff could review and copy those documents;
(2) the original account books to Plaintiff so that Plaintiff could
review those documents.

b. For litigation fees.

B. THE SECOND STATEMENT OF CLAIMS

Plaintiff: **Deep Doo Doo Inc.**

The 1ˢᵗ Defendant: Sino-US Yunnan Auto Technological Services
Limited
The 2ⁿᵈ Defendant: Mr. Wong
The 3ʳᵈ Defendant: Wong Member 2
The 4ᵗʰ Defendant: Wong Member 3
The 5ᵗʰ Defendant: Wong Member 4

With respect to the above named Defendants, Plaintiff Deep Doo
Doo Inc. alleges the following:

**1. Plaintiff holds 95% of the shares of Sino-US Yunnan Auto
Technological Services Limited (hereinafter "the JV"), thereby in
accordance with Article 25 of the Rules for the Implementation
of the Law of the PRC on Chinese-Foreign Contractual Joint
Ventures (hereinafter "Rules for the Implementation") Plaintiff is
entitled to have six seats in the JV's Board of the Directors.**

a. As a majority shareholder, Plaintiff holds 95% shares of the JV
The JV is a Sino-Foreign Cooperative Joint Venture formed by the
1st defendant (it was named "Sino-US Yunnan Auto Technological
Services Limited" at that time) and Plymouth Corporation,
(hereinafter "Plymouth"), and Ken Li on Month, Day, 2005
(Evidence 1: Business License). The respective portion of shares
owned by each of them is: Sino-US Yunnan Auto Technological
Services Limited: 67.75%, Plymouth: 27.25%, and Ken Li: 5%.

According to Article 10.2 of the Articles of Association of the JV (Evidence 3), the JV's board of the directors shall be composed of seven directors, out of which four shall be appointed by the 1st defendant and the other three shall be appointed by the 2nd defendant. Thus, the 1st defendant appointed the 2nd defendant the chairman of the JV's board of the directors, the 3rd defendant, the 4th defendant, and the 5th defendant the directors. Plymouth appointed Ted the vice-chairman of the board of directors, and appointed Michael and Scott directors.

On Month, Day, 2005 Plaintiff became one of the two shareholders of Defendant by acquiring all the shares held by Plymouth and Ken Li and most of the shares held by the 1st defendant through three Share Transfer Agreements (Evidence 4, 5, and 6). After these transactions, Plaintiff holds 95% of the shares of Defendant, and Sino-US Yunnan Auto Technological Services Limited holds 5% of the shares of Defendant (Evidence 7and 8).

On January, Day, 2006, the (Government Agency) ("GOVT") accepted the JV's application to modify the registration of shareholders (Evidence 9: Approval of Modification to the Registration issued by GOVT), and the JV obtained the renewed Business License (Evidence 10). After that, there are two shareholders of the JV. One is Plaintiff which holds 95% the shares, and the other is Sino-US Yunnan Auto Technological Services Limited which holds 5%.

b. According to Article 25 of Rules for the Implementation, Plaintiff is entitled to have six seats in the JV board of the directors

Article 25 of the Rules for the Implementation: "The board of directors or the joint management committee shall be composed of not less than three members, and their distribution shall be determined through consultation by the Chinese and foreign parties with reference to the investment or conditions for cooperation contributed by each party."

In accordance with this provision, the exact number of the directors in a contractual joint venture appointed by each party shall depend on the parties' respective investment proportion. Therefore, with 95% of the shares Plaintiff is entitled to appoint six directors.

On Month, Day, 2007, Plaintiff once informed the JV and the 1st defendant that the number of Plaintiff's seats on the board of the directors should add up to six and the number of the 1st Defendant's seats should be cut down to one. Meanwhile, Plaintiff appointed directors of the JV (Evidence 11: Plaintiff's information).

Afterwards Plaintiff learned that on Month, Day, 2005 the day when the 1st defendant, Plymouth and Ken Li transferred their shares in the JV to Plaintiff, the 1st defendant forged four documents on the modification of composition of the JV's board of the directors (Evidence 12) in conspiracy with the 2nd defendant, the 3rd defendant, the 4th defendant, and the 5th defendant. The 1st defendant then used these forged documents to modify the registration of composition of the board of directors on Month, Day, 2006. Because of these illegal acts, Plaintiff had only one seat on the JV's board of directors now (Evidence 9: Approval of Modification to the Registration issued by GOVT).

2. In accordance with the law, the four documents forged by five defendants should be declared null and void

Resolution A: The Resolution on Amending the JV contract,
Resolution B: The Resolution on Amending the JV's Articles of Association
Resolution C: The Resolution of the 2nd Meeting of First Board of Directors of the JV on appointment and dismissal of the directors
List : The List of the Directors of the JV

All the forged documents above were made on December 12, 2005.

Document	Content	Signatory	True or False
Resolution A	Reduce Plaintiff's seats of the JV board of directors to one and add up 1st defendant's seats to four	The 2nd defendant, Michael	False
Resolution B	Reduce Plaintiff's seats of the JV board of directors to one and add up 1st defendant's seats to four	The 2nd defendant, Michael	False
Resolution C	1. The 1st defendant appointed the 2nd defendant, the 3rd defendant, the 4th defendant, and the 5th defendant directors of the JV; 2. Plaintiff appointed Scott vice-chairman of the board of the directors; and	The 2nd defendant, the 3rd defendant, the 4th defendant, the 5th defendant, Michael, Ted, Scott	False
List	Reduce Plaintiff's seats of the JV board of directors to one and add up defendant's seats to four	The 2nd defendant, the 3rd defendant, the 4th defendant, the 5th defendant, Scott	False

3. These four forged documents are in breach of Article 29 of the Rules for the Implementation, thereby they should be declared null and void.

4. Five defendants fraudulently violated Plaintiff's right as a majority shareholder by forging the above four documents, thereby they should compensate for the losses suffered by Plaintiff

5. Wherefore, Plaintiff pays judgment against Defendant as follows:

  a. For declaring the Resolution on Amending the JV contract, the Resolution on Amending the JV's Articles of Association, the Resolution of the 2nd Meeting of First Board of Directors of the JV on appointment and dismissal of the directors and the List of the Directors of the JV null and void.
  b. For [$—], the compensation for Plaintiff's losses resulted from the five defendants' illegal acts.
  c. For litigation fees.

C. The Third Statement of Claims

Plaintiff: **Deep Doo Doo Inc.**

The 1st Defendant: Sino-US Yunnan Auto Technological Services Limited_
The 2nd Defendant: Mr. Wong
The 3rd Defendant: Wong Member 2
The 4th Defendant: Wong Member 3
The 5th Defendant: Wong Member 4

With respect to the above named Defendants, Plaintiff Deep Doo Doo Inc. alleges the following:

1. As a majority shareholder, Plaintiff holds 95% of the shares of Sino-US Yunnan Auto Technological Services Limited (hereinafter "the JV").

2. Defendants breached their fiduciary duty to the JV by running businesses competing with the JV.

a. Defendants have run businesses competing with the JV.

- o   Defendants have run Wong & Sons Trade Co., of which the business competes with the JV.
- o   Defendants have run Wong Specialty Automotive Services, of which the business competes with the JV.

b. According to Article 149 of the Company Law, Defendants breached their fiduciary duty to the JV by running businesses competing with the JV and shall repay the profits resulting from the breach to the JV.

c. According to Article 150 of the Company Law, Defendants shall compensate the JV for the damages and losses caused by such breach.

3. Defendants breached their fiduciary duty to the JV by embezzling the assets of the JV.

a. Defendants embezzled the assets of the JV.

b. According to Article 117 of the General Principles of the Civil Law, Defendants shall restore the assets embezzled to the JV.

c. According to Article 148, Article 150 of the Company Law and Article 117 of the General Principles of the Civil Law, Defendants shall compensate the JV for the damages and losses caused by such embezzlement

4. Defendants breached their fiduciary duty to the JV by forging four documents to amend the organization of the Board of Directors of the JV.

a. In Month, Day, 2005, Defendants forged four documents to amend the constitution of the Board of Directors of the JV

b. Defendants deceived the (Government Agency) (hereinafter "GOVT") by submitting the forged documents to apply for amending the registration of the constitution of the JV's Board of Directors

c. The above fraudulent acts of Defendants breached their fiduciary duty to the JV

5. In accordance with Article 152 of the Company Law, Plaintiff is entitled to sue Defendants on behalf of the JV.

6. WHEREFORE, Plaintiff prays judgment against Defendant as follows:

a. For injunctive relief prohibiting Defendants from running business competing with the JV;
b. For repaying the profits that Defendants have earned from competition to the JV;
c. For restoring the assets embezzled by Defendants to the JV;
d. For damages and losses caused by the breach of fiduciary duty committed by Defendants; and
e. For litigation fees.

After receiving no response to either request, in late fall 2007 we filed the first lawsuit; at least that's what we tried to do. Unfortunately, when we arrived at the appropriate government office, the clerk turned us away, explaining that the court was not accepting ANY new legal filings until further notice due to a heavy caseload. Our attorney informed us that we would have no choice but to wait until the caseload eased and the court again opened its docket to new claims. And there was no indication of when that might be; it could be a few days or a few months, our attorneys told us.

Finally, nearly two months later, the first statement of claims was accepted by the judge in the Case-Acceptance Division of the court in the district where AutoStar had been headquartered. Unfortunately, Liu & Liu erred in presuming that this was the court that had jurisdiction over our case. Shortly after we filed, Mr. Gao received a call from the court informing him that the court with which we had filed had no jurisdiction over the lawsuit and referred us to a court in a different district. As instructed, we filed the case with the new court. After waiting nearly two more weeks, we were informed by the court that if the case had merit, we would be issued a notice of acceptance. Nearly three months later, we were notified that our case was accepted.

Shortly afterward, we received a *Summons and Notice of Members of the Collegiate Bench* (the collegiate bench consists of three judges and a court clerk, all of which were named in the documents we received) from the Beijing First Intermediate Court. On the date and time specified in the summons, we would have our first evidence-exchange proceeding. The court also notified us that they had sent a statement of claims and other judicial documents to AutoStar by mail. We were all happy that after so many long and tedious months of gathering documents and speaking with the attorneys, our case was finally moving forward.

When the day of the first court proceeding finally arrived, we were told by Mr. Gao that we shouldn't expect a great deal to be accomplished. The normal procedure on the first day, he told us, was that the judge would listen to arguments from both sides and determine what would be admissible based on what he heard. As it turned out, however, the court heard only from our side because no one from Mr. Wong's side bothered to show up. Mr. Gao said that this also wasn't unusual, particularly in cases like ours. As a result, however, we were told that the court could not make a ruling until Mr. Wong was given every opportunity to present his case. Before we left, the court set a second date approximately one week later to give Mr. Wong's side another opportunity to present a response to our claims. If Mr. Wong's side didn't show up for this hearing, I fully expected to receive a default judgment against him.

It was during this time between court dates that Mr. Gao suggested we make an amendment to our first statement of claims. We knew that according to Article 34 of China's Company Law, we were entitled to have access and make a copy of the articles of association, resolutions of the board of directors, and the financial statements and accounting ledgers of AutoStar. Unfortunately, we later learned that according to this law, we were not entitled to many other documents, such as tax invoices, vouchers, and most importantly, company bank records. Because we felt that having access to the banking records was essential if our side hoped to prevail, Mr. Gao amended our first statement of claims to include the additional documents we needed. In doing so, he cited several precedent-setting cases in which the court agreed to a plaintiff's request for additional records and documentation.

We returned to court for our second hearing at the time set by the judge. Mr. Gao initiated the proceedings by presenting our amended statement of claims to the court. Again, because no one from Mr. Wong's side appeared at the appointed time, I expected the judge to issue a summary default judgment against him. I also expected that the court would approve our amendment and enter an order entitling us to the requested information. I was stunned to find out I was wrong on both counts. In fact, despite the fact that Mr. Wong failed to appear without explanation, the court gave him an *additional* thirty days to reply to the amendment we filed; the court, we were told, would take responsibility for providing notification. Without the amendment we likely would have received a default judgment but would not have been entitled to the additional documents we needed.

While a month may not seem like a long time, I'm sure it was the longest thirty days Tom could remember. Despite the apparent progress, Tom grew increasingly impatient as ABC Capital continued to bleed cash. While ABC was funding the lawsuit, it continued to fund AutoStar so it wouldn't become insolvent and plunge into bankruptcy. If AutoStar failed, Tom knew it was unlikely that ABC Capital would ever be able to recover any meaningful portion of its investment. If anyone mentioned a word about China to Tom, his face flushed and his blood pressure immediately rose. His first experience in China had been a disaster, and he had no intention of ever investing another dime in China or in any Chinese company. To him, Chinese businesspeople couldn't be trusted. He would never make another investment in any foreign firm unless Western culture and *rule of law* applied. But I didn't agree with Tom's thinking, and I still don't. I've completed a number of transactions in China. In these the companies prospered, the investors prospered, and the shareholders prospered. Moreover, the CEOs I've dealt with have been the polar opposites of Mr. Wong. In my opinion, failure was caused by Tom receiving a favorable report on Mr. Wong and the proposed joint venture (as Mr. Wong had done nothing of this nature in the past), probably providing a false sense of security in both; lack of experience and oversight by the law firm; and outright fraud. In the time since AutoStar, I've learned from my other Chinese business experiences. Sometimes, I'm surprised at myself when I find myself now *thinking* Chinese.

As an example of how my understanding of the Chinese way of doing business has helped me, I would like to relay a short story. During a recent contract negotiation with a company CEO, I came to a final, largely ceremonial meeting prepared to sign a contract. All of the tough negotiations were behind us; the meeting was supposed to be nothing more than a formal signing ceremony. We were there to ink the deal. Just before taking our seats, the company's attorney breezed into the conference room. A hushed silence enveloped the room as the attorney and CEO huddled together, speaking in a seemingly urgent manner.[48] After a few moments, the CEO broke from his huddle and, through our interpreter, apologized, telling us his attorney felt it was important to make a few minor changes to the agreement. Although I was outwardly calm, I was inwardly seething at being blindsided by this last-second stunt. As the attorney led a review of the ten amendments to the contract, some minor and some not, I didn't say a word. When the attorney finished, everyone turned toward me, eager to see my reaction. I began by apologizing to the CEO, saying that I thought I had provided him with enough time to review the document and suggest changes. I continued, telling him to take more time and to review it with his attorney more carefully; I would be back in a month or two, and we could discuss it by e-mail in the meantime. "Take your time. I'm really in no great hurry," I assured him.

Although I wasn't in a particular hurry, I knew by now from my growing portfolio of experience in China that the CEO was eager to immediately make the deal. After all, I represented his link to money, and he wasn't about to let me walk away that day. He'd never let me leave the meeting without signing the agreement—and I knew it. As I began to pick up my belongings to prepare to leave, the CEO quickly huddled again with his attorney; then he asked the attorney to leave the room. As the attorney

---

[48]   I firmly believe that this huddle between the CEO and the corporate attorney was arranged long before I entered the conference room on that day.

shut the door on his way out of the conference room, the CEO walked over to me, reassuringly grasped my arm, and, through my interpreter, asked me to stay, telling me that in his opinion, his attorney had given him poor advice. "Of course we will sign the original agreement!" he exclaimed. "No changes are necessary!" he laughingly bellowed. A few moments later we finished signing the contracts, and I was on my way. I have traveled back to that company on business on numerous occasions since that day, and I never once saw that attorney again. The company performed as advertised.

My point in relaying this story is that understanding Chinese businessmen and the Chinese way of doing business is critical to success in China. It is absolutely possible for Westerners to be successful and make money, but it's critical to understand how. Although we failed to find success in the AutoStar deal for several reasons, the overarching problem is that Tom's Chinese partner was basically a crook, and there were no legal restrictions placed on him or the company that prevented him from acting in a fraudulent way. There were no checks and balances.

Let's get back now to our story. During the time we were preparing for our lawsuit, AutoStar was no longer generating any revenue, so it was essential that Ted slash costs, and he did. He started by laying off the few employees still working for our side of the business, including himself and Jonathan. Tom also made me the acting CEO of the company. I assumed this role without any compensation whatsoever. I simply wanted to do what I could to help Tom and ABC Capital recover as much of the money Mr. Wong had stolen as possible. During this period, as only a true friend would, Scott stayed on to assist me by handling any remaining accounting and check writing and by helping me to produce and compile information we needed for the case. Scott did this without any complaint or compensation; he was there only to support me.

It was late July 2008, and the end of the thirty-day period the court provided to Mr. Wong approached. On the morning of the hearing, I fully expected Mr. Wong to be a no-show once again. Instead, the court itself didn't show; a clerk called our attorney just hours before the hearing to cancel, explaining that the judge was ill and that it would be necessary to postpone the proceedings until he regained his health. Since the three-week-long Beijing Olympics would begin in just over a week, I knew that it would be at least a month before the hearing could be rescheduled.

More than a month later, in September 2008, we finally had our hearing. As I suspected, neither Mr. Wong nor his attorneys bothered to show up. Our attorney, Mr. Gao, again asked the court to grant our motion and compel Mr. Wong to provide us with the documents we had requested. Although the court had been in possession of our amendment for nearly two months at this point, the judge responded that he would study our amendment and make a ruling in a "short time" (no period of time specified). He continued, saying that although courts in some jurisdictions provide plaintiffs with access to original copies of documents, he did not view this as the rule. As a result, he said that he would need more time to study our request. "Yeah, right," I thought as Maria interpreted the judge's response. I'd been in China long enough to know that probably wasn't the real reason. What he was really saying, I presumed, was that because the case has been filed by a foreign firm, he had to be cautious in his rulings because a spotlight would be focused on his decisions, so he wanted to carefully consider our request.

Approximately six weeks later, the court finally provided its response. They ruled that since AutoStar, the defendant, had not attended any of the hearings as required in the summons, the court would render a default judgment in our favor. The judgment stipulated that AutoStar must, within three days of coming into force, provide its original articles of association, all resolutions of the board of directors, and all of its financial statements to us for review and duplicate. The court denied our request for access to AutoStar's original accounting records, dismissing this portion of our claim.

Mr. Wong was given thirty days to appeal the judgment before it came into force. The court informed us that if AutoStar did not comply with the requirements of the judgment, we could apply to China's judicial enforcement division to compel compliance. In this situation, the enforcement division sends an enforcement notification to the defendant, giving them a specific period of time to voluntarily comply with the judgment. If AutoStar failed to comply within the designated time frame, we were told that the enforcement division would appoint a judge to accompany us to AutoStar and order the documents be provided to us.

We were elated. We finally succeeded in Chinese court with our first statement of claims. I passed the news along to Tom, who was happy to finally be able to relate positive legal progress to his partners. During our conversation it seemed as if the burden on his shoulders suddenly eased somewhat, judging by the fact that he was more conversational than he had been in quite some time.

A couple of weeks later, Mr. Gao called to inform us that AutoStar refused to receive the judgment being served by the court. However, he said that according to the rules of Chinese civil procedure, the judgment was still regarded as being successfully served on AutoStar even though they didn't technically receive it. Mr. Gao also told us that during the process of serving the judgment, the court discovered that AutoStar was in the process of moving out of its offices to some other undisclosed location. Once again, Mr. Wong was thumbing his nose at us. "While you may think you have won by receiving judgment against me," I could imagine him saying, "good luck trying to find me to collect on it."

At this point, in early November 2008, it was becoming increasingly clear that the odds we would ultimately prevail against Mr. Wong were growing longer by the day. First, and most importantly, we had run out of money. Our legal bills had been mounting for months, and, because of that, Liu & Liu refused to spend another minute on our case until they received payment. Second, we had no idea where Mr. Wong had relocated his operations, and to find him we'd have to hire a private investigator. To make matters worse, ABC Capital ignored my calls and e-mails asking them for additional funds to continue the enforcement action and file the second statement of claims. Finally, we had only thirty days left until our officers and directors liability insurance policy expired, and the clock was ticking. Without that protection, the members of the board—including me—would be forced to resign.

Because the end seemed imminent, all of us on the board drafted our resignation letters and busied ourselves with the task of preparing to discontinue our involvement with AutoStar by making the proper notifications. Scott and I began by compiling a checklist of tasks we needed to accomplish to make sure we didn't leave any loose ends when we closed shop. We met with the attorney to go over the checklist to ensure we didn't leave anything out. Because Tom continued to ignore any e-mails I sent him, we decided that Scott would call him to reaffirm that he knew the directors and officers insurance would expire in less than thirty days and that without the insurance and additional funding we would be forced to close the doors. Two days after Scott placed the call, I received an e-mail from ABC indicating that they still wanted to move forward with our legal action and asking me to prepare an estimate of the costs of continuing the lawsuit for the next three months.

When I compiled the budget, I included paying Liu & Liu in full. Our outstanding legal bill with them at the time was more than $40,000, and Mr. Gao bluntly told me the last time I met with him that if we didn't pay what we owed, they wouldn't spend another minute on our case. Without Liu & Liu's assistance, we had no chance of proceeding, prevailing, or collecting our claim. They were the single most important player on our team.

I e-mailed the budget to ABC Capital and let a week pass before I called them to get their reaction and ask them when they would wire the additional funds. Instead of telling me that "the check is in the mail," however, they informed me that their in-house counsel wanted to set up a conference call with Liu & Liu to discuss the case. It was immediately obvious to me that ABC wanted to make sure they had a winnable case and a good shot at recovering at least a portion of their investment before they proceeded any further.

The next day I set up the conference call between Liu & Liu and ABC's counsel for the following evening (8:30 p.m. EST, which corresponded to 9:30 a.m. the next day Beijing time). ABC provided the call-in number, and, at the appointed hour, Liu & Liu and I were on the line. Unfortunately, ABC's counsel didn't pick up the call. During the more than thirty minutes we waited, Liu & Liu and I discussed the case, the weather in Beijing, and anything else we could think of until it became obvious that ABC wasn't going to show.

Early the following morning I e-mailed Tom but received no reply; quite frankly, I really didn't expect one. By the end of 2008, a substantial decline in global equity markets took a toll on the value of ABC Capital's investment portfolio. Long-standing and revered Wall Street brokerage firms were closing their doors. The biggest US and international banks were being forced to merge or go out of business. Bernie Madoff, one of Wall Street's most revered investment personalities, was unveiled as a fraud and Ponzi scheme perpetrator, and investors everywhere were holding onto their cash. ABC had obviously thrown in the towel on AutoStar and was focusing on the impact of the global financial markets implosion on its business. By then, AutoStar was literally the last thing on their minds. It was clear that ABC Capital had decided to cut its losses with AutoStar and redirect its resources.

With no additional funds forthcoming from ABC Capital, just before Christmas 2008 every member of the board submitted resignations. Mr. Wong kept all of ABC's money as well as all of the equipment, cars, and other assets still in his possession. The judgment was never enforced, and Liu & Liu was never paid the $40,000 they were owed. And ABC Capital lost its entire investment.

On my next flight to Beijing a few weeks later, a friend of mine who was a manager at a major New York–based hedge fund was seated directly across from me. Unsurprisingly, he was on his way to China to speak to several Chinese companies about investing in them. "Nothing changes," I thought. China is still the Wild, Wild East and, just like the Wild, Wild West, there's great opportunity, and the rules are still being written.

I'd like to finish this chapter by providing an update about the lives and careers of the characters I've introduced you to throughout this story, starting with myself.

Once the transaction went sour, in January 2009 ABC Capital filed a lawsuit to recover its investment, naming me the CEO of the shell company (Deep Doo Doo) to replace Mr. Wong. To be honest, there wasn't a long line of suitors eager to assume that job. In fact, I didn't want the job at all either. But it was clear that next to Mr. Wong, I knew more about the business and transaction than anyone, and Tom needed me to run the company and act as a liaison with the new litigation attorneys to have any chance at all of recovering ABC's investment. After all, I thought, "How much work could it be to run a company with no employees and with the law firm handling the litigation?" Boy, was I wrong about that!

As soon as the lawsuit began to move forward, I found myself devoting so much time to the company and lawsuit that I was lucky to get five hours of sleep a night. The process was pure drudgery, involving endless hours of tedious work. Initially, I didn't expect the long hours necessary to prepare for the lawsuit. Once I outlined the events and provided the documentation that led to the lawsuit, I assumed my time devoted to the case would be limited to answering a few questions now and then. Instead, it seemed that the attorneys constantly required additional information and answers to a seemingly endless list of questions. I did it, and I'm still glad I did.

In the meantime, my consulting business in China was growing rapidly. I signed contracts with a growing portfolio of Chinese client firms that needed my assistance in helping them to raise foreign capital. Because I was so busy, every hour I devoted to AutoStar was siphoning time away from my business—and money out of my pocket. It quickly became a burden, but if I walked away then there would never be a chance to proceed with the lawsuit. No one else was willing to put in the time for free. However, by the summer of 2009, Tom and ABC finally pulled the plug on the lawsuit. They realized that the odds of collecting a dime from Mr. Wong were about as good as winning a Powerball Power Play. That allowed me to now focus on my business.

While my AutoStar experience was a disaster, overall my life became more interesting, and I've had incredible success in China since that first trip to Beijing so many years ago. I'm grateful to this day that I didn't let one bad person keep me from doing business in China. Because of the lessons I learned from that experience, I have become a very successful Western businessman in China by adhering to the *Chinese way* of doing business. I've found that if I adhere to the rules I've described in this book, I can minimize problems in my negotiations and have more successful results with Chinese clients. Of course, I still encounter problems from time to time. That's part of business and is to be expected. But my experience, coupled with the rules I've outlined, have replaced the years of pessimism with financially rewarding relationships with savvy, honest, and hard-working Chinese businessmen.

Today I have a rapidly growing and profitable China consulting practice that provides due diligence services for a great many financial institutions. My growing list of friendships and relationships with Chinese officials has also provided me with an expanding inventory of Chinese corporate clients that have a desire to secure foreign capital and enter the public markets. As far as I'm concerned, the greatest business opportunities in the world today are in China. I am confident that if you follow my rather simple rules and commit them to memory, you'll have a great chance at being successful in business in China. But if you go into China like so many others, thinking that your knowledge of doing business in the United States or other Western countries is all you need, you'd be just as well off taking a trip to Las Vegas. At least in Vegas, you'll have some fun while you're losing your money.

Tom is still a managing partner at ABC Capital and is doing quite well despite the catastrophic collapse that plagued the markets and ruined many investment firms in 2008 and 2009. Although, to the best of my knowledge, Tom hasn't invested again in individual Chinese companies, I suspect he realizes that Mr. Wong and AutoStar do not accurately reflect the goodness and character of the Chinese people and the tremendous investment opportunities available there. He is fully aware that many firms that have invested in China have been very successful and knows he owes it to his shareholders to take another look.

Ted is now the CFO of a US company and lives back in the States, where he gets to spend more time with his two lovely daughters. His new company is involved in putting together a fund. Since he returned to the States, Ted and I have had more than one opportunity to share a glass of Scotch and a cigar and talk about China. He believes the future is clearly there, but he's done with traveling and wants to spend whatever time he has watching his daughters grow and mature. And who can blame him?

Jonathan works with me and runs the due diligence team in China. He only occasionally drives me crazy. He performs due diligence on

Chinese companies for our institutional clients and travels considerably throughout China. I am pretty sure that Jonathan will likely get married in the near future as he seems to have found his match in Shanghai, where he now resides.

Scott and I continue to work together inside and outside of China. Like me, Scott believes strongly in the opportunities available in the Chinese market.

Mr. Wong's nephew, Mr. Li, still continues to suffer for helping us with AutoStar. Because Mr. Li wanted to do the right thing and sided with us against his uncle, Mr. Wong used Mr. Li's credit cards to run up $50,000 in charges at hotels and restaurants and to make other purchases. After maxing out his cards, Mr. Wong gave the cards back to Mr. Li, who now owes the bank this money with no hope of repaying it. Despite his problems with his uncle, Mr. Li is currently doing well and works for me on several of my other China projects. He's making money and, for the first time in a while, and has begun to enjoy life again.

Maria continues as an indispensable assistant for everything I do in China. She prepares business plans, organizes financial data, and translates and explains documents to both American and Chinese clients. She is the best interpreter I have ever met and is as good as any executive assistant I've worked with. Maria has received nearly a dozen job offers for more money than I pay her. So far, she has turned these opportunities down because her position offers great personal fulfillment and because leaving the rest of us now would be like leaving a family.

Ken Li is still working for his uncle at their orchard farm on Hainan, and I see him every so often.

David is still at Global Accounting in Hong Kong, and I still work with him on other projects in China. Mr. Wong still owes him nearly $200,000 for the accounting and audit work he performed. Obviously, it is very unlikely that he'll ever collect a penny.

Vera recently left Global Legal and joined another large Beijing-based law firm. When she left, the managing partner at Global Legal tried to collect about $250,000 in past-due billings from ABC Capital. At first, Tom offered to work out a settlement with Global Legal, but he quickly discovered that Vera had provided absolutely no information on the invoices detailing how much time she spent, on which days she provided services, and on what activity she worked. She lumped all of her and her associate's hours together, along with the billing rates, and sent them to us. Despite continued requests, none of that detail was provided, and so Tom refused to pay, and we never heard from the law firm's managing partner again.

CHAPTER 10

Lessons

While I sometimes don't agree with various aspects of the *Chinese way* of doing business, I don't for an instant believe that Mr. Wong represents the average Chinese businessperson—and you shouldn't either. In fact, since my first experience with AutoStar, I've met and worked with hundreds of Chinese business professionals, business owners, and public officials. In general, I have found the vast majority of these individuals to be smart and tough but also very thoughtful, kind, and wonderful hosts. However, I cannot overemphasize the importance of understanding Chinese culture, Chinese businessmen, and the Chinese way of doing business to achieving success in China.

It is my hope that by sharing my experiences, this book will provide the reader with a better understanding of how to successfully exploit all of the potential that China has to offer. I believe China offers exceptional opportunities for making money, and I believe these opportunities will continue to exist for at least another decade. During China's long and ancient history, its people have been merchants to the world. To an average Chinese person, it doesn't matter if you're from Germany, Brazil, Japan, Italy, or the United States—they are very anxious to do business with foreign firms from any country. They want our money, they want our technological expertise, and they want to build business relationships. It is my strong belief that if you follow the lessons I've detailed in Refkin's Rules, you'll be better prepared to succeed and achieve your goals when doing business in China.

I summarize Refkin's Rules here again for your convenience.

Refkin's Rules for doing business in China:

Refkin's Rule #1: Remember the importance of "face." In China, always remember the importance of "face" in the conduct of all of your personal and business relationships. Maintaining face is important in Chinese social relations because face translates into power and influence and affects goodwill. It is critical to avoid losing face or causing the loss of face at all times.

Refkin's Rule #2: At dinner, always remember that you're the "main course." In China, business banquets and dinners are an extremely important part of the business process. The most important thing for foreign businessmen to understand about these events is that they are always the "main course."

Refkin's Rule #3: The Chinese always have a game plan, and the plan is always all about money. The primary objective of Chinese businessmen who do business with foreign business partners is to extract as much money as possible as soon as possible. All other plans or objectives are simply icing on the cake. Chinese businessmen always have well thought-out and detailed game plans—and those plans always center on money.

Refkin's Rule #4: There is never an exception to Refkin's Rule #3 (The Chinese always have a game plan, and the plan is always all about the money). No elaboration required.

Refkin's Rule #5: The boss never approaches you directly. He almost always uses an intermediary. When doing business with foreign partners, the "boss" (CEO/leader) on the Chinese side rarely approaches the foreign business leader directly. The boss almost always uses an intermediary for everything from initial contacts to negotiation to conveying news.

Refkin's Rule #6: Expect the unexpected. When doing business in China, always expect the unexpected. There are always exceptions to any rule.

Refkin's Rule #7: Expect short time frames in which to think and act where money is concerned. Whenever foreign businessmen are to provide capital to Chinese businessmen, the Chinese always minimize the period between when the request is made and delivery is due. Chinese businessmen never give the foreign partner long to think about the delivery of funds.

Refkin's Rule #8: Expect to get the "bad news" from a "friend." Chinese businessmen will relay "bad news" to foreign business partners only as a last resort, and usually by utilizing a friend or someone the foreign partner likes or feels comfortable with. Once the foreign business partner does get the bad news, it is always relayed at the last possible moment to allow for the least amount of time for the foreign partner to think and to act.

Refkin's Rule #9: When putting a business deal together, be prepared to foot the bill. When doing business in China, Western businessmen should be prepared to foot the bill. Chinese businessmen will never spend any of their own money if they can help it—they'll spend yours.

Refkin's Rule #10: In China, nepotism rules. For Chinese businessmen, family is supremely important. In many Chinese businesses, the boss's wife and adult children often not only have a large stake in ownership but in management as well. If you think your business relationship will trump the Chinese family relationship, you're wrong.

Refkin's Rule #11: When doing business in China, leave nothing to chance. When doing business with Chinese businessmen, foreign business partners should never assume anything. Be sure to get all of the details of your contracts translated and signed by people you trust.

Refkin's Rule #12: Evasiveness is a culturally acceptable Chinese business tactic—expect it. Chinese businessmen will never directly answer a question where the outcome is not favorable to them. Evasiveness is not only an acceptable but an expected and strategic business tactic. Chinese businessmen want flexibility to achieve a favorable outcome. A direct, unfavorable response will take away that flexibility.

Refkin's Rule #13: When doing business with a Chinese partner, you have to continually prove your value to the relationship to remain in the deal. As soon as your Chinese partner knows that no additional money or value will be provided, your leverage in the transaction is gone, and the terms of the partnership will likely change.

Refkin's Rule #14: When doing business In China, you're always dealing with "the government." When dealing with medium to large Chinese companies, foreign business partners should always assume they are dealing with the government. The government (local, provincial, national, or all three, depending on size and significance) always is involved in international business partnerships. The challenge for the foreign business partner is to understand how.

Refkin's Rule #15: When doing business in China, expect that contracts and agreements are only a start. If you think you're going to do business with the Chinese on the strength of the deal alone, you're wrong. Winning a bid or inking a deal doesn't mean you've succeeded or hit a home run; it simply means that you've gotten to first base. Once the contract has been signed and the ceremony is over, make sure your attorney directly files any relevant paperwork, rather than relying on your partner to do so.

Bibliography

Amato, Ralph. "Reverse Shell Mergers Explained: Everything You Wanted to Know about Reverse Shell Mergers." http://reverseshellmerger.com/category/china/. Accessed July 18, 2008.

Big Four (audit firms). See the Big Four Wikipedia profile page at http://en.wikipedia.org/wiki/Big_Four_(audit_firms). Accessed May 1, 2011.

Cantonese. See its Wikipedia profile at http://en.wikipedia.org/wiki/Cantonese. Accessed May 1, 2011.

CFA Institute: The Global Association of Investment Professionals. https://www.cfainstitute.org/Pages/index.aspx Accessed May 1, 2011.

China. See its Wikipedia profile page at http://en.wikipedia.org/wiki/China. Accessed May 1, 2011.

China Central Television (CCTV). For more information, see its Wikipedia profile page at http://en.wikipedia.org/wiki/China_Central_Television. Accessed May 1, 2011.

Chinese New Year Holidays. See its Wikipedia profile at http://en.wikipedia.org/wiki/Chinese_New_Year. Accessed May 1, 2011.

Culture Shock. See its Wikipedia profile at http://en.wikipedia.org/wiki/Culture_shock. Accessed May 1, 2011.

Federal Accounting Standards Advisory Board (FASAB). http://www.fasab.gov/accepted.html. Accessed May 1, 2011.

Folta, Paul H. "Cooperative Joint Ventures: Savvy foreign investors may wish to consider the benefits of this flexible investment structure," The China Business

Review Online, http://www.chinabusinessreview.com/public/0501/folta.html. Accessed May 1, 2011.

"GRE Test Change, Why Always Targets at Chinese Students?" *China People Daily, P.R. China*. Wednesday, August 14, 2002. http://english.peopledaily.com .cn/200208/14/eng20020814_101472.shtml. Accessed August 29, 2008.

Great Hall of the People or Rénmín Dàhuìtáng (人民大会堂). See its Wikipedia profile page at http://en.wikipedia.org/wiki/Great_Hall_of_the_People. Accessed May 1, 2011.

Great Wall of China. See its website at http://www.greatwall-of-china.com/. Accessed May 1, 2011.

Guanxi. See its Wikipedia profile at http://en.wikipedia.org/wiki/Guanxi. This page was last accessed on May 1, 2011.

Initial Public Offering (IPO). See the Wikipedia profile page at http:// en.wikipedia.org/wiki/Initial_public_offering. Accessed May 1, 2011.

Kwintessential. http://www.kwintessential.co.uk/resources/global-etiquette /china-country-profile.html. Accessed May 1, 2011.

Liao, D. and P. Sohmen. 2001. "The Development of Modern Entrepreneurship in China." *Stanford Journal of East Asian Affairs*, spring, Vol. 1

Micropaint Repair System. See http://www.micropaint.net. Accessed May 1, 2011.

Mid-Autumn Festival. See its Wikipedia profile at http://en.wikipedia.org/wiki /Mid-Autumn_Festival. Accessed May 1, 2011.

OTC Pink. http://www.otcmarkets.com/otc-pink/home. Accessed May 1, 2011.

Public Company Accounting Oversight Board (PCAOB). See its website at http://pcaobus.org/Pages/default.aspx. Accessed May 1, 2011.

Renminbi. See its Wikipedia profile at http://en.wikipedia.org/wiki/Renminbi. This page was accessed May 1, 2011.

Ring Roads of Beijing. See the Wikipedia profile page at http://en.wikipedia.org /wiki/Ring_roads_of_Beijing. Accessed May 1, 2011.

Securities Exchange Guide to Microcap Stocks. http://www.sec.gov/investor /pubs/microcapstock.htm. Accessed May 27, 2008.

Shimek, L. and Y. Wen. 2008. "Why Do Chinese Households Save So Much?" International Economic Trends, Federal Reserve Bank of St. Louis. http://research. stlouisfed.org/publications/iet/20080801/iet.pdf. Accessed May 1, 2011.

Standing Committee of the National People's Congress. http://en.wikipedia.org /wiki/Standing_Committee_of_the_National_People's_Congress. Accessed May 1, 2011.

Term Sheet. See its Wikipedia profile at http://en.wikipedia.org/wiki/Term_sheet. Accessed May 1, 2011.

U.S. Securities and Exchange Commission. http://www.sec.gov/. Accessed May 1, 2011.

Work Unit (danwei). See the Wikipedia profile at http://en.wikipedia.org/wiki /Work_unit. Accessed May 1, 2011.